Ten-Minute Math Mind-Stretchers

Quick Problems and Activities to Help Reinforce Essential Math Skills

by Laurie Steding

SCHOLASTIC
PROFESSIONAL BOOKS

New York ☆ Toronto ☆ London ☆ Auckland ☆ Sydney

DEDICATION

To my family of math whizzes, Bob, Sarah, and Danny, and to all my students, past and present, for opening my eyes to the wonderful world of math.

Cover design by Jaime Lucero
Cover photographs copyright © by Photodisc
Interior design by Jaime Lucero and Robert Dominguez for Grafica, Inc.
ISBN 0-590-86563-3

Table of Contents

INTRODUCTION

What tremendous strides math education has made in the past ten years! There is so much information to share with children, and so little time to fit more into our already over-scheduled days. That's why this book was written—to give students a ten-minute taste of math problems, to make them think hard for a short period of time, and to stimulate their curiosity about concepts they may not have thought of as math concepts.

ABOUT THE PROBLEMS

All the problems in this book correspond to the NCTM Standards and are designed to supplement a well-rounded math curriculum. A sample activity is shown below to show you what each problem includes.

Each chapter also includes an "Across the Curriculm" section which describes more elaborate activities designed to help students realize that math is everywhere.

The level of difficulty varies within each chapter, keeping gifted students challenged and giving students who may not yet have grasped a concept alternative ways to approach it.

Because students come to us with a variety of skills; they will notice that some problems may seem difficult, while others may seem easy. The problems and activities in *Ten-Minute Math Mind-Stretchers* will give students opportunities to demonstrate their strengths as well as opportunities to explore and practice skills that need strengthening. Since students learn well from each other, many of the problems and activities

A reference to the Standard number or numbers it addresses (see section on NCTM Standards).

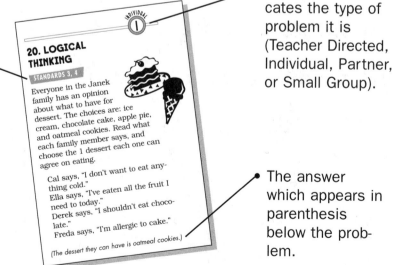

An icon which indicates the type of problem it is (Teacher Directed, Individual, Partner, or Small Group).

The answer which appears in parenthesis below the problem.

are designed to be done with a partner or with a small group of students.

Although the problems and activities in this book take only a short period of time to do, it is important to spend time after each one to discuss the reasoning and strategies students used to arrive at their answers. Providing an environment in which children discuss, demonstrate, and justify their mathematical thinking will encourage them to take some intellectual risks and expose them to new ways of doing math.

The problems and activities in *Ten-Minute Math Mind-Stretchers* can be used at the beginning or end of each day, during transition times, or to provide a lively introduction to the math period. Many of the problems could be done for homework as well, but you want to be sure to discuss the answers in class.

Enjoy using this book to stretch your students' minds a bit each day, and to help them see that math is fun!

NCTM STANDARDS

The National Council of Teachers of Mathematics published 13 standards that the council considers essential to any elementary math curriculum. The following is a brief discussion of the essence of each standard. Each problem in *Ten-Minute Math Mind-Stretchers* includes the number or numbers (1 to 13) of the Standards it supports. What follows is a brief description of each standard:

1. MATHEMATICS AS PROBLEM SOLVING: The ability to apply mathematical skills confidently and meaningfully to unfamiliar situations is the goal of math instruction.

2. MATHEMATICS AS COMMUNICATION: Reading, writing, modeling, drawing, and discussing are all important tools in helping children to explore, convey, and clarify mathematical concepts and ideas.

3. MATHEMATICS AS REASONING: Giving children opportunities to analyze, draw conclusions, and justify their thinking helps them gain a sense of self-reliance and confidence in their mathematical abilities and helps them see that mathematics makes sense.

4. MATHEMATICAL CONNECTIONS: Helping children see how concepts and ideas in one area of math relate to other areas of math, other subject areas, and their everyday lives fosters an appreciation of the usefulness of mathematics.

5. ESTIMATION: Developing and practicing estimation skills increases children's flexibility in using numbers, equips them with additional skills to apply in reasoning, increases the number and types of situations in which they apply math skills, and helps them recognize that the study of mathematics is more than finding exact answers.

6. NUMBER SENSE AND NUMERATION: By understanding the meaning of numbers, number relationships, and the effects of operations on numbers, students can make sense of the way numbers are used in the real world.

7. CONCEPTS OF WHOLE NUMBER OPERATIONS: Understanding the properties of addition, subtraction, multiplication, and division, knowing when and how to use the operations, and comprehending how the operations relate to one another is the basis for computational skill.

8. WHOLE NUMBER COMPUTATION: Acquiring proficiency with the operations of addition, subtraction, multiplication, and division is essential in enabling students to solve problems. Computation methods include paper and pencil and mental math, as well as calculator and computer.

9. GEOMETRY AND SPATIAL SENSE: The ability to recognize 2- and 3-dimensional shapes, their properties, the relationships among shapes, and to know the effects of changes on shapes helps children understand and describe the physical world around them.

10. MEASUREMENT: Students learn and practice measuring to strengthen and formalize their intuitive comparisons of length, width, height, capacity, weight, mass, area, volume, time, temperature, and angle.

11. STATISTICS AND PROBABILITY: Collecting, organizing, describing, displaying, and interpreting data, as well as exploring concepts of chance, give students opportunities to investigate and analyze the world around them.

12. FRACTIONS AND DECIMALS: An understanding of fractions and decimals greatly expands students' knowledge of the number system and their appreciation of its usefulness in describing the real world.

13. PATTERNS AND RELATIONSHIPS: The ability to identify patterns and regularities in events, shapes, designs, and sets of numbers, and to describe them mathematically, broadens children's skill base for organizing and analyzing information from the world around them. It also strengthens children's association of mathematics with finding regularities.

Math Sense

1. MATH ON THE JOB

`STANDARDS 4, 6`

Have children, working in pairs, list 5 ways that a pizza delivery person uses math in his or her job. Have pairs share their ideas in a class discussion.

(Answers will vary, but may include: calculating time, distance, and cost; finding addresses; making change; keeping track of hours worked; packaging food.)

2. MATH IN SPORTS

`STANDARDS 4, 6`

List 3 ways a member of a swim team uses math. Compare your list with your partner's. How many different ways do you have altogether?

(Answers may vary, but may include: timing races, calculating speed, comparing scores, calculating scores, determining depth; total number of ways will vary from 3 to 6.)

3. USING MATH IN WEATHER FORECASTS

`STANDARDS 2, 4, 6`

What math words does a weather forecaster use when he or she talks about the weather? Make a list. Listen to a radio or TV weather report and add to your list any math words the forecaster uses that aren't already on your list.

(Lists will vary, but may include: words relating to temperature—degrees Fahrenheit, degrees Celsius; time of weather changes or duration of storms—hours, overnight; wind speeds—miles per hour; predicted or actual measures of rain or snow—inches, feet; probability—percent chance.)

4. COMPARING AND ORDERING SPORTS SCORES

`STANDARDS 4, 6`

Have children, working in pairs, write down 5 different sports and make up possible game scores for each. Then ask them to write the sports in order from greatest number of points in a game to least number of points. Have pairs share what they wrote.

(Sports and scores will vary. Possible sports and their score order: basketball, football, volleyball, baseball, soccer.)

5. MAKING MATH SENSE

STANDARDS 2, 4, 6

Fredric likes to exaggerate when he talks. Work with the other members of your group to rewrite each exaggeration of Fredric's below so that it is believable.

   a. I was on an airplane that flew across the country in 15 minutes!

   b. I only need 1 hour of sleep every night!

   c. Last night it rained 17 inches in my backyard!

(Answers will vary, but possible responses may include: a. I was on an airplane that flew across the country in 8 hours; b. I only need 7 hours of sleep every night; c. Last night it rained 2 inches in my backyard.)

6. MAKING MATH SENSE

STANDARDS 2, 4, 6

A new announcer on the radio made this report: "A bank robber got away from the First National Bank with 5000 cents. He escaped in a car which sped away at 70 feet per hour. Police set up a roadblock on Main Street

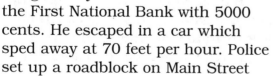

and captured the crook. Now, we'll pause for a commercial break. We'll continue this story in 1 year." Which 3 words in the story do not make sense? Write each word and the word you would change it to so the story makes sense.

(Change cents to dollars; change feet to miles; change year to minute.)

7. COMPARING WAYS TO TRAVEL

STANDARDS 2, 4, 5

Sally, Tania, Marcus, Toshio, Sarah, and Jaime are having a race to find out who can travel around the block the fastest. They each travel a different way: Sally saunters, Tania trots, Marcus marches, Toshio tiptoes, Sarah strides, and Jaime jogs. Write their names in the order you think they will finish the race.

Compare your answer with your partner's. Discuss why you wrote them in the order you did.

(Accept reasonable answers. Trotting and jogging are generally faster than striding and marching, which in turn, are faster than sauntering or tiptoeing. One possible response: Tania, Jaime, Sarah, Marcus, Sally, Toshio.)

8. MAKING A SCHEDULE

STANDARDS 2, 4, 10

"Make sure you allow yourself enough time so that you're not late for school today," said Juan's mom. Work with your partner to list the things Juan probably needs to do in the morning before school. Beside each item on your list, write the amount of time you think it should take Juan to do.

How much time will it take him to do all the things on the list? If he needs to leave for school at 8:00 to be on time, what is the latest time Juan can get up?

(Lists will vary, but may include: get dressed, eat, wash, and collect homework. Times will vary, but the time it takes him to do everything on the list, when added to the time he needs to get up, should bring the time to 8:00.)

ACROSS THE CURRICULUM

Math Mobiles (Art)

Each student needs 2 copies of the Math Vocabulary sheet on page 16, crayons or markers, a stick or hanger, scissors, string, and glue. Discuss what each of the vocabulary words means and have students give examples.

Give children the following instructions to make the mobiles:

1. Decorate the words on each copy of the Math Vocabulary sheet and cut the words apart.
2. Glue 2 words that match from each sheet back to back, with pieces of string or yarn in between, hanging 2 or 3 words on each string.
3. Tie the strings to the stick or hanger, placing them so the mobile balances.

Note: You may want to omit or add vocabulary words so that the mobiles more closely reflect children's vocabulary level.

Math Words Scavenger Hunt (Language Arts)

Distribute copies of the Math Vocabulary sheet on page 16 to small groups of students or individuals. Instruct students to:

1. Look for the words on the sheet in math books, newspapers, magazines, on TV, or on signs around their neighborhoods.
2. Record where each one is found and copy the sentence in which it is used.

Allow students a few days to look for the words. Set aside some time for them to share their findings.

9. COMPLETING A WORD PROBLEM

STANDARDS 2, 12

Write a question to complete this word problem:

Amber and her sister went to the store to buy hats. Amber bought a hat that cost $4.50. Amber's sister bought a hat on sale for $3.95.

Trade problems with your partner and solve. Check each other's work.

(Questions will vary, but may include: How much did the two hats cost altogether? or, How much more did Amber pay for her hat than her sister?)

10. CALCULATING COSTS

STANDARDS 3, 4, 6

"The wind knocked part of my fence down," groaned Ms. Kamveris, "and it's going to cost a lot of money to fix it."

 What does Ms. Kamveris need to know before she can figure out how much it will cost to repair the fence?

(Accept reasonable responses. One possible response: She needs to know the length and height of the section of the fence that needs to be repaired, how much each foot of fencing costs, and how much it will cost to pay somebody to put in the new fencing if she cannot do it herself.)

11. MEASURING TIME

STANDARDS 6, 10

List these situations in order from shortest to longest amount of time it seems you spend waiting:

–waiting to get a drink of water from the fountain
–waiting for food in a restaurant
–waiting for a birthday or special holiday
–waiting for a bus
–waiting your turn in a game

Compare your list with your partner's. What is the same about your lists? What is different?

(Lists will vary.)

12. COMPARING SALE PRICES

STANDARDS 6, 12

Ana went to the mall to shop for jeans. She found 1 pair that was on sale for 1/3 off the regular price, and another pair that was on sale for 1/4 off the regular price. Write the steps Ana needs to follow to find which pair of jeans has the lower price.

(Answers may vary. One possible answer: Find out the regular price of each pair of jeans. Divide by 4 the pair whose price is 1/4 off, then subtract that amount from the regular price. Divide by 3 the pair whose price is 1/3 off, then subtract that amount from the regular price. Compare the 2 sale prices.)

13. USING COUPONS TO SAVE

STANDARDS 4, 6, 10

Willy's mom said if he clips coupons for things they need to buy, and helps her shop, he can keep all the money saved by using the coupons. List 5 things that they might buy using coupons. How can Willy keep track of how much money is being saved?

(Lists may vary. Ways Willy can keep track may vary, but may include: He can look at the store receipt, identify the coupon deductions, and find the sum of all the deductions.)

14. NUMERICAL PREFIXES

STANDARDS 2, 6

Tell how these words are related:

triple play   tripod   triplets
tricycle   trio   triathlon

What are some words that mean *2* of something? Draw a picture for each word.

(They all mean three of something; Words for two may vary, but may include: pair, bicycle, biathlon, double play, double dip, twins; Check students' drawings.)

15. WRITING WORD PROBLEMS

STANDARDS 2, 6

Which is greater—the number of years of bad luck that Superstitious Sam has if he breaks a mirror, or the number of lives his black cat has?

Write a math problem like this one.

(The answer is the number of lives his black cat has—the 9 lives of a cat is greater than 7 years of bad luck. Problems will vary.)

Math Work (Social Studies)

Ask students to interview relatives and neighbors to find out how they use math in their jobs. Make a class chart of the information they gather.

16. DAYS, MONTHS, AND SEASONS

STANDARDS 4, 5, 6, 10

Drifting on a raft in the middle of the ocean, a man spent over 120 days alone before being rescued!

Work with your partner. About how many months is 120 days? What season was it 120 days ago? List 4 things that you have done or that have happened to you during the last 120 days.

(120 days is about 4 months. Season will vary; lists will vary.)

17. VENN DIAGRAMS

STANDARDS 2, 11

Make a Venn diagram with 2 intersecting circles. Label one circle *Me* and the other circle with the name of a member of your family. In the circle labeled *Me*, list characteristics that describe you, but not your family member. In the other circle, list characteristics that describe your family member, but not you. In the space where the circles intersect, list characteristics you both share.

(Venn diagrams will vary.)

18. VENN DIAGRAMS

STANDARDS 4, 9, 11

Make a Venn diagram with 3 intersecting circles. Label the circles *Bumpy*, *Round*, and *Small*. Write the following words in the circle or intersection where they belong. (Some objects may not belong in any circle.)

orange	marble	bulletin board
clock	apple	dictionary
cookie	tree	thumb tack
dice	roll of	
	paper towels	

(Venn diagrams may vary. Accept reasonable responses.)

19. PERSONALIZED VENN DIAGRAMS

STANDARDS 2, 4, 9, 11

Make another Venn diagram. Decide on the categories, such as *Dogs* and *Cats*, and label the circles. Write characteristics in the circles, such as *meows* for cats and *barks* for dogs. In the area where the circles intersect write shared characteristics, such as *four-legged*. Show your Venn diagram to the members in your group and see if they can add any characteristics to it.

(Check students' Venn diagrams.)

20. LOGICAL THINKING

STANDARDS 3, 4

Everyone in the Janek family has an opinion about what to have for dessert. The choices are: ice cream, chocolate cake, apple pie, and oatmeal cookies. Read what each family member says, and choose the 1 dessert each one can agree on eating.

Cal says, "I don't want to eat anything cold."
Ella says, "I've eaten all the fruit I need to today."
Derek says, "I shouldn't eat chocolate."
Freda says, "I'm allergic to cake."

(The dessert they can have is oatmeal cookies.)

21a. FOLLOWING DIRECTIONS

STANDARDS 2, 6

Have children draw pictures according to the following instructions:

- If you are older than 8 years, draw a sun high up in the sky.
- If you are 8 years old or younger, draw the sun low in the sky.
- If you are a boy, draw several butterflies on your paper.
- If you are a girl, draw several birds on your paper.
- If your birthday is on an even-numbered day, draw flowers.
- If your birthday is on an odd-numbered day, draw trees.
- If you have more than 4 people in your family, draw fish in a pond.
- If you have 4 or fewer people in your family, draw rabbits in the grass.

Have children add details to their pictures to complete them, if you wish. Display all the finished pictures. Have students describe what the pictures show about the class and each student in particular.

21b. WRITING DIRECTIONS

STANDARDS 2, 6

Have children work in small groups. Challenge each group to write a set of instructions for drawing pictures. Suggest that they use 4 or more categories, such as hair color, length of

name, whether or not they have a pet, whether or not they like to eat nachos, and so on. Have groups trade instructions and draw pictures. Have groups check each other's drawings.

(Answers will vary.)

22. ESTIMATING QUANTITY

STANDARDS 5, 11

Have children take handfuls of dried beans (or popcorn kernels, or paper clips, for example) and estimate how many of each they think they can scoop in one handful. Have students record their estimates and then count the actual number of beans, etc. Ask how close their estimates were to the actual amount they could hold.

(Answers will vary.)

23. MAKING AND ADJUSTING ESTIMATES

STANDARDS 4, 5

Choose a book without many pictures on the pages. Open the book and look at one of the pages.

a. Write an estimate of how many words you think are on the page.
b. Count the number of words in the first line of the page, and the number of lines on the page. Estimate the total number of words again, using this information.

c. Is this estimate different from your first estimate?

d. Now count the words to find the actual word count. Which estimate was closer to the actual word count?

(Estimates will vary; number of words on pages will vary. Either estimate may be closer to the actual number, but it is most likely that the second estimate will be closer, since it is based on more information.)

24. FINDING NEEDED INFORMATION

INDIVIDUAL
1

STANDARDS 4, 5, 11

What information would you need to know in order to make a good estimate of the number of school lunches that will be eaten by the students in your school today?

(Answers may vary. Possible answers include:

A C R O S S   T H E   C U R R I C U L U M

○ ☆ ○ ⌐ ○✦ ○ ☆ ○ ⌐ ○ ✦ ○ ☆ ○ ⌐ ○ ○ ☆ ○ ⌐ ✦ ○ ☆ ○ ⌐ ○ ○ ☆ ○ ⌐✦ ○ ☆ ○

Find the Secret Number (Logical Thinking)

Have children play this game in small groups. Each group needs a red, yellow, and green crayon or marker. One player writes a number and the other players try to guess it, using clues which the number-writer gives them.

How to Play:

1. Player A writes a 3-digit number, keeping it hidden from the other players.
2. Player B writes down a guess.
3. Player A responds to the guess by drawing 3 dots, color-coded as follows: A yellow dot means that 1 of the digits is correct, but it is in the wrong position.
   A green dot means that 1 of the digits is correct and is in the correct position.
   A red dot means that neither the digit nor the position is correct.
   (It's important to understand that the order of the dots does not correspond to the order of the digits in the number.)
4. Player C then uses this information to write down another guess.
5. Play continues with players guessing and Player A responding until the correct number is guessed.

For example:
Player B: Guesses the number 356.
Player A: Draws a red dot, green dot, and yellow dot to indicate that 1 digit is not correct in either number or position, 1 digit is correct in both number and position, and 1 digit is correct in number, but not in position.
Player C: Guesses the number 362.
Player A: Draws a red dot, green dot, and green dot to indicate that 1 digit is not correct in either number or position, while 2 digits are correct in both number and position.
Player D: Guesses the number 367.
Player A: Tells them it's the correct number.

the number of people who usually eat the school lunch, the school lunch menu, the day's attendance figure.)

SMALL GROUP
S

25. THINGS THAT COME IN DOZENS

STANDARDS 2, 4, 6

Work with 2 or 3 other students to brainstorm things that are grouped or packaged in sets of 12. Draw or list them. What do you notice about your list?

(Answers will vary, but may include: eggs, bagels, donuts, cookies, muffins, inches; students may notice most or all of the items in their lists are food items.)

INDIVIDUAL
I

26. WEATHER FORECASTS

STANDARDS 2, 5, 11

What information do you use to help you predict what the day's weather will be like when you get up in the morning? Why is knowing the day's weather forecast helpful? Write a story about how you had to change your plans for the day based on a weather forecast.

(Answers may vary, but may include: weather forecasts on the radio, TV, or in the newspaper; the look and feel of the weather when you look or step outside. Knowing the weather forecast helps you decide what to wear and what to do that day. Stories will vary.)

ACROSS THE CURRICULUM

Estimation Station (Estimating Capacity)

Create an "Estimation Station" in an area of the classroom. In it, display a see-through container filled with some items such as dried beans or blocks. Vary the item or quantity from day to day. Children can take turns being in charge of the Estimation Station and bring in objects and containers from home. Each day, have students write an estimate of how many objects are in the container. At the end of each day, count the objects together. Determine who gave the closest estimate. Encourage children to discuss estimation strategies they used.

Suggested objects:
pencils, marshmallows (both large and small), dry cereal, dry pasta, marbles, rocks, dried beans, seeds, shells, blocks, pennies, rice, peanuts, jelly beans

Math Vocabulary Words

equivalent	fewer	greater	sum	difference
more	less	total	product	percent
under	over	between	equal	value
capacity	increase	average	range	about

CHAPTER 2

Addition and Subtraction

1. A FAIRY TALE ADDITION PROBLEM

STANDARDS 2, 8

How many animals would there be altogether if the bears (but not Goldilocks) invited the pigs (but not the wolf) and the billy goats (but not the troll) over for a party? Draw a picture to show your answer.

Write a problem of your own that uses numbers from stories. Trade problems with your partner. Draw a picture to show the answer.

(3 + 3 + 3, or 9, animals. Check children's drawings.)

2. ADDING POINTS

STANDARDS 4, 8

Suppose colors were assigned the following points:

purple = 6 points   red = 5 points
green = 4 points   yellow = 3 points
blue = 2 points   white = 1 point
(Other colors are worth 0 points)

Look at your clothing. Count each color only once in each piece of clothing. Add the points. What is your color point total?

Make up your own color point system and add up your points again. How does your new total compare with your first total?

(Totals will vary; color point systems will vary. New totals can be greater, less, or the same as the first totals.)

3. ADDING POINTS

STANDARDS 2, 6, 8

Suppose each letter of the alphabet is worth points. The letter A is worth 1 point, B is worth 2 points, C is worth 3 points, and so on, up to Z, which is worth 26 points. Make a table to show how many points each letter is worth.

Add up the letters in your name using the points in the table. Then add up the letters in your partner's name. We did one for you below.

S U S A N

19 + 21 + 19 + 1 + 14 = 74

A=1   B=2   C=3   D=4   E=5
F=6   G=7   H=8   I-9   J=10
K=11 L=12 M=13 N=14 O=15
P=16 Q=17 R=18 S=19 T=20
U=21 V=22 W=23 X=24 Y=25
Z=26

*(Totals will vary; First names with the greatest
and least number of points will vary.)*

4. SUBTRACTING FROM PICTURES

`STANDARDS 4, 8`

Draw a picture of the American flag
the way it is now. How many states
are there in the United States? Look
at the early American flag shown
below. How many colonies were
there in 1776? How many more
states than colonies do the flags
show?

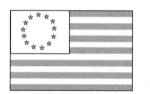

(50; 13; 50 - 13, or 37 more states.)

5. ILLUSTRATING AND WRITING A WORD PROBLEM

`STANDARDS 1, 2, 8`

Think of an addition problem that
has 14 as its sum. First draw a picture of the problem, then write it as
a word problem.

(Illustrations and problems will vary.)

6. ADDEND PAIRS FOR 100

`STANDARDS 7, 8`

Work with the other members of
your group to write all the different
combinations of 2 whole numbers
that add up to 100. What strategies
did you use to find them? Compare
your strategies with another group's.
Did your groups use the same ones?
Explain.

*(0 + 100, 1 + 99, 2 + 98, 3 + 97, . . .
50 + 50. Strategies will vary. Possible strategies include: to begin with combinations of
numbers ending in 0, such as 10 + 90; finding
a pattern such as 100 + 0, 99 + 1, 98 + 2,
and so on; thinking of dollars and cents: 25 +
75, 50 + 50; Groups may or may not have
used the same strategies.)*

7. WRITING NUMBERS

`STANDARDS 3, 6, 8`

Use the digits 2, 4, 5, and 8 to write
two 2-digit numbers whose sum is
100. Write 2 possible answers.

*(The 2 possible answers are 48 + 52 and
58 + 42.)*

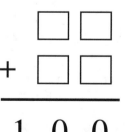

Addition Stones (Sports and Recreation)

This is a Native American game. For playing pieces you will need 4 smooth stones. Draw each of the simple designs shown below on one side of each stone. The other side of each stone remains blank.

Any number of children can play. Players take turns placing the stones in a container, shaking the container, and spilling the stones onto a hard surface. They receive points for each design showing, according to the chart below. They add the points for their total score. The player with the greatest score after 3 rounds wins.

Blank side of stones = 0 points
Moon = 5 points
Star = 10 points
Sun = 15 points
Snowflake = 20 points

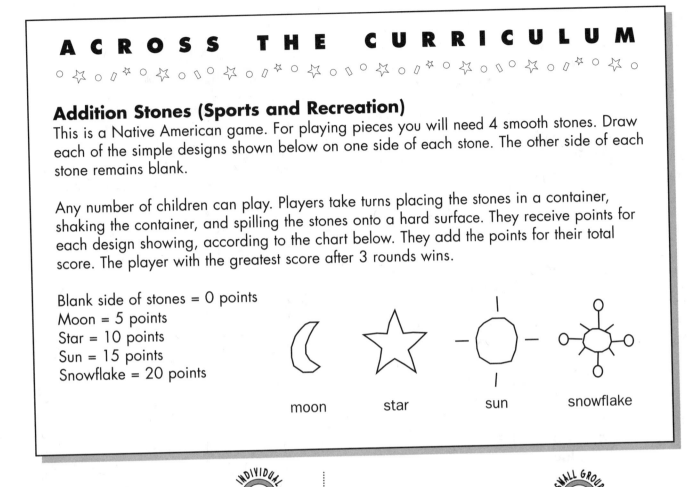

moon   star   sun   snowflake

---

8. USING MENTAL MATH

STANDARDS 3, 8

Use mental math to find the answer to each question. Tell what strategy you used for each one.

  a. What number comes after
     17 + 8?
  b. Which is greater, 21 + 11 or 20 + 14?
  c. What is 68 + 42?

(26; 20 + 14; 110; strategies may vary.)

9. WRITING ADDITION SENTENCES FOR THE NUMBER 50

STANDARDS 7, 8

Write 10 addition sentences for the number 50. You can have as many addends in each addition sentence as you'd like. For example, 10 + 10 + 10 + 20 = 50.

Compare your number sentences with the sentences of other members of your group. How many different number sentences does your group have altogether? Do you think there are still more addition sentences you could write for the number 50? Explain.

(Number sentences will vary; group totals of number sentences will vary. Children should realize that there are many more addition sentences that can be written for the number 50.)

10. ADDITION RULES

STANDARDS 6, 8, 13

Copy and complete each sentence below to write 4 addition rules.

    a. The sum of an odd number and an odd number is always _____.

    b. The sum of an even number and an even number is always _____.

    c. The sum of an odd number and an even number is always _____.

    d. If you change the order of the addends, the sum _____.

Discuss your rules with your partner. Work together to write 2 examples of each rule.

(a. The sum of an odd number and an odd number is always an even number; b. The sum of an even number and an even number is always an even number. The sum of an odd number and an even number is always an odd number; d. If you change the order of the addends, the sum remains the same. Examples will vary.)

11. DETERMINING POINTS FOR A SCORE

STANDARDS 7, 8

Look at the target (page 25). In 3 rounds, throwing once each round, Harry got 37 points and Kim got 42 points. Write a number sentence to show the number of points Harry got on each turn to get that total. Write a number sentence to show the number of points Kim got.

(Order of addends in number sentences may vary: Harry—25 + 10 + 2 or 25 + 7 + 5; Kim—25 + 10 + 7.)

12. AN ADDITION GAME

STANDARD 8

Play a target game using the target (page 25) and 4 small, light objects, like dry pasta. Place the target flat on a table, chair seat, or on the floor. Take turns with your partner closing your eyes and dropping the pasta onto the target area. Add the points of the sections in which the pasta lands. The player with the greatest number of points after 3 rounds wins.

(Scores will vary.)

13. SUBTRACTING MONEY

A girl's mom said that each time the girl didn't have her daily chore done by supper time, 10¢ would be subtracted from her allowance of $2.25 a week. At the end of the week, the girl received $1.85 for her allowance. How many times was she late doing her chore?

Explain to your partner how you got your answer. Did you solve it the same way as your partner? Explain.

(4 times; solution methods may vary. Possible strategies include: Count up by dimes from $1.85 to $2.25—$1.95, $2.05, $2.15, $2.25. So, the answers is 4 times; or write an equation—$2.25 - $1.85 = $0.40, to find the amount subtracted, then determine the number of dimes in $0.40—4 dimes, so the girl was late doing her chore 4 times.)

14. ADDING AND SUBTRACTING MONEY

Grapes and strawberries cost $1.00. The grapes cost 10¢ less than the strawberries. Use mental math to find the price of each snack. Explain how you got your answer.

(The grapes cost 45¢ and the strawberries cost 55¢. Explanations may vary but may include: Use the guess and check strategy. Start with both items priced at 50¢. Subtract 10¢ from the strawberries to get the price of the grapes, which is 40¢; 50¢ + 40¢ = 90¢. 90¢ is too low. Add 5¢ to each price; 55¢ + 45¢ = $1.00. Check: 55¢ - 45¢ = 10¢. That's it!)

ACROSS THE CURRICULUM

Exercise Equations (Sports and Recreation)
Make a class list of the 10 most popular exercise movements, such as touching toes or twisting at the waist. Specify a number of repetitions and assign points to each exercise. For example, deep knee bends (5 times)—10 points. Post the list so everyone can see it.

Have children working in small groups create short (3-5 minute) exercise routines consisting of exercises listed in the chart. Each group can teach the rest of the class its routine, and children can write number sentences to find how many points the routine is worth. Ask children questions such as, "How could you change the routine so the total number of points is 10 points less? 10 points greater?"

15. SUBTRACTING COOKIES

STANDARDS 6, 8, 12

Linda's aunt made 2 dozen cookies. She told Linda and her cousins not to eat more than half of the cookies. Linda ate 4 cookies, Michael ate 3 cookies, Caroline ate 6 cookies, and little Kelsey ate 2 cookies. Did they eat more than half the cookies? Explain.

(Yes. One possible explanation: 2 dozen cookies is 24 cookies. Half of 24 is 12. Linda and her cousins ate 4 + 3 + 6 + 2, or 15 cookies. 15 is greater than 12.)

16. COMPARING EXPRESSIONS

STANDARDS 3, 6, 8

Without subtracting, compare these two expressions:

335 – 49   497 – 72

Which expression has the greater number for an answer? How do you know? Discuss it with your partner. Did you both solve it the same way?

(497 – 72. Answers may vary. One possible response: Look at the numbers in the tens places. In the first expression, 3 is less than 4, so regrouping is needed. The answer will have a 2 in the hundreds place. In the second expression, 9 is greater than 7, so no regrouping is needed. The answer will have a 4 in the hundreds place. The answer to the second expression is greater than the answer to the first expression.)

17. WRITING ABOUT SUBTRACTION

STANDARDS 2, 4, 8

Have students work in pairs to write news articles about their class. The article must include at least 1 subtraction situation. For example, students might write: On Thursday, 17 of Mrs. Chung's 30 fourth graders brought their lunch to school. The other 13 students ate the school lunch of macaroni and cheese.

Compile all the news articles into a class newspaper and have students give it a title, such as "The Subtraction Gazette."

(News articles will vary.)

18. DRAWING A PICTURE TO SOLVE A PROBLEM

STANDARDS 2, 8

Julie bought a bag of 28 marbles at the store. When she got home she discovered there was a hole in the bag, and only 9 marbles were left! How many marbles did Julie lose between the store and home? Draw a picture of Julie's walk home from the store, and show where all the missing marbles might be. Trade pictures with your partner and find all the missing marbles.

(19 marbles; check students' drawings. There should be 19 marbles hidden in each picture.)

19. DRAWING A PICTURE TO SOLVE A PROBLEM

STANDARDS 2, 6, 13

The Cardinals Mighty Sluggers baseball team has 11 players. The team's uniforms are red. At one game, 7 players wore red socks. Three of the players with red socks were also wearing red sweatshirts. Draw a picture to answer the following questions:

a. How many were not wearing red socks or sweatshirts?

b. How many were not wearing red socks?

c. How many were not wearing red sweatshirts?

Write a subtraction sentence for each answer.

(Check students' drawings; a. Four players were not wearing red socks or red sweatshirts—11 – 7 = 4; b. Four players were not wearing red socks—11 – 7 = 4; c. Eight players were not wearing red sweatshirts—11 – 3 = 8.

20. USING INFORMATION IN A TABLE TO SOLVE A PROBLEM

STANDARDS 3, 7, 8

Ms. Kember's class is baking cookies as a special treat. They need to decide what kind of cookies to make. Of the 26 students in the class, 3 students dislike chocolate chip cookies. Also, 18 students like cookies with raisins, 20 students like sugar cookies, and 12 students dislike ginger cookies. Make a table showing how many kids like and dislike each kind of cookie. What do you think the class should do?

(Chart should resemble one below. Decisions will vary, but may include: Make 2 different kinds of cookies; make chocolate chip cookies since the fewest number of students dislike it.)

Cookie Type	# Who Like It	# Who Don't Like It
Chocolate Chip	23	3
Cookies with Raisins	18	8
Sugar Cookies	20	6
Ginger Cookies	14	12

21. WRITING ADDEND PAIRS

STANDARDS 7, 8, 13

Complete the Number Buddies chart (page 26). Write 2 numbers on each T shirt that, when added together, equal the number of that row. For example, in the row labeled *6* you can complete the number buddies to show *6 + 0, 0 + 6, 5 + 1, 1 + 5,* and so on.

(Order of expressions may vary, but each row should include some of the following:

Row 0: 0 + 0
Row 1: 1 + 0, 0 + 1
Row 2: 2 + 0, 0 + 2, 1 + 1
Row 3: 3 + 0, 0 + 3, 2 + 1, 1 + 2

Row 4: 4 + 0, 0 + 4, 3 + 1, 1 + 3, 2 + 2
Row 5: 5 + 0, 0 + 5, 4 + 1, 1 + 4, 3 + 2, 2 + 3
Row 6: 6 + 0, 0 + 6, 5 + 1, 1 + 5, 4 + 2, 2 + 4, 3 + 3
Row 7: 7 + 0, 0 + 7, 6 + 1, 1 + 6, 5 + 2, 2 + 5, 4 + 3, 3 + 4

A C R O S S   T H E   C U R R I C U L U M

Marvelous Machines (Science)

Explain to students they are going to invent machines! Have children work in small groups to brainstorm and decide what task their machine will perform. Then have them draw the machine, making sure to include parts from the list below, and calculate the total cost of their machines. Each group can present its drawing to the class, explaining what the machine does and the cost. The class can create award categories such as most interesting machine, least expensive machine, machine with the most parts, and so on. They can then vote or identify which group receives each award.

Price List

Wheels . . . . . 40¢
Long boards . $1.50
Short boards . 75¢
Dials . . . . . . 65¢
Wires . . . . . . 50¢
Tubes . . . . . . 35¢
Lights . . . . . . 80¢

Addition Target

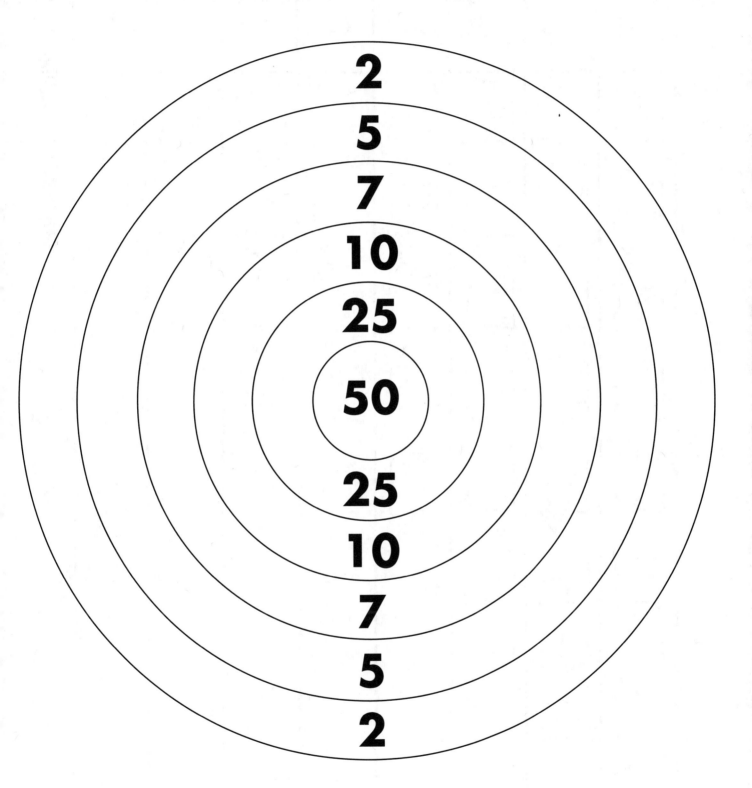

Number Buddies

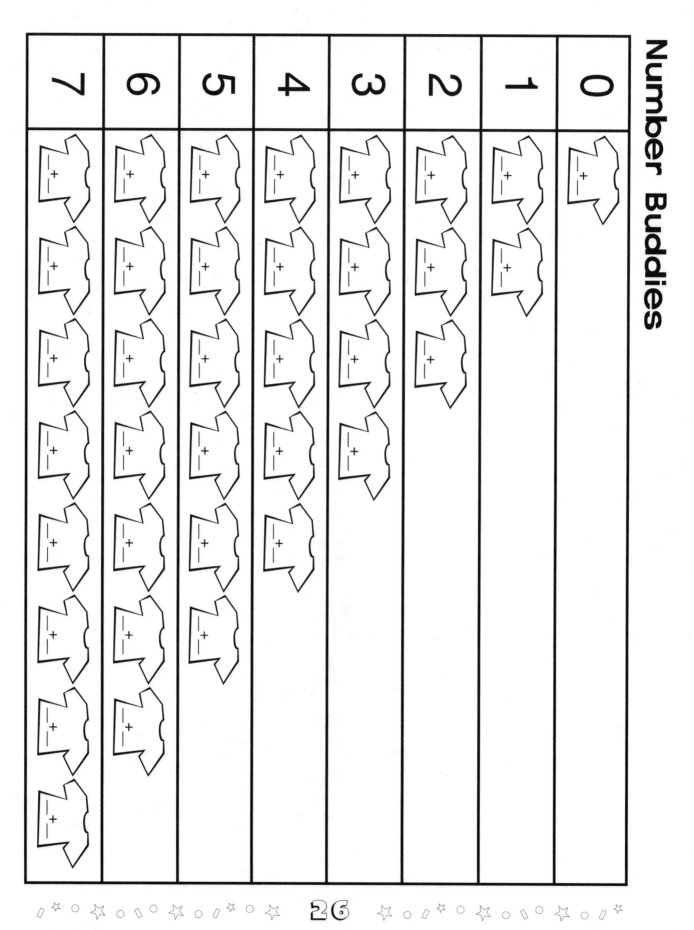

Number Lines and Place Value

1. VISUALIZING NUMBER LINES

STANDARDS 6, 9

Ask students to picture a number line in their minds. Ask them to start at zero and mentally move along the number line as you count the following numbers: 1, 2, 3, 4, 5, 6, 7, 8, 9.

Ask them to go back to zero and to now imagine themselves skipping over the even numbers and landing on the odd numbers. Have them count aloud as they skip: 1, 3, 5, 7, 9, 11. Ask them to continue "skip counting" until they reach the next odd number that

a. has the same digit in both the tens and the ones places.
b. is greater than 40, and has a number in the tens place that is 5 less than the number in the ones place.

Continue giving students clues for numbers to find along their number lines. Encourage students to think of clues to give their classmates as well.

(a. 33; b. 49)

2. USING CLUES AND A NUMBER LINE TO FIND A NUMBER

STANDARDS 6, 9

Picture a number line from 0 to 30 and then use these clues to find the mystery number:

a. It is between 15 and 20.
b. It's an odd number.
c. It's closer to 15 than to 20. Write the number.

Write some clues of your own for 3 different mystery numbers. Trade clues with your partner and write the numbers.

(17; mystery number clues will vary.)

3. ADDING AND SUBTRACTING ON A NUMBER LINE

STANDARDS 2, 8, 9

Ask students to picture a number line in their minds. Give them the following instructions:

a. Start at 2.

b. Move ahead 5.
c. Go back 3.
d. Move ahead 4.

Have them identify the number at which they've stopped. Ask them to write a number sentence to describe how they moved along the number line.

(They've stopped at 8; 2 + 5 - 3 + 4 = 8.)

4. DESCRIBING NUMBERS

STANDARDS 3, 6

Work with 2 or 3 other students. Use the numeral cards (page 32). Take turns choosing 2 numeral cards and giving 2 clues as to what the numerals are. The clues can, for example, describe how far apart the numbers are on a number line, whether they are odd or even, what the sum would be if they were added together, and so on. A third clue can be given if the number is not guessed in one round.

For an additional challenge you can choose 3 cards to make one 2-digit number and one 1-digit number, or 4 cards to make two 2-digit numbers.

(Numbers chosen and clues given will vary.)

On the Number Line (Physical Education)

This game can be played with a large or small group of students. One player is the caller. The other players pretend they are standing on number lines (so they need to leave plenty of space on either side of them). The caller identifies the number players are to start on. Then the caller calls out another number, and the players move the number of steps to the left or right necessary to put them on the new number. The caller continues, calling out other numbers for players to move to along their number lines. Players take turns being the caller.

You may also have the caller call out the number of steps to take, and in which direction, and have players tell on what number that puts them.

5. WRITING GREATEST AND LEAST NUMBERS

STANDARDS 3, 6

Use the numeral cards (page 32) and take turns choosing 3 cards. The person who chose the cards uses the digits to write the greatest number he or she can. The other person uses the same digits to write the least number he or she can.

Continue until you've each written 5 numbers. Write all 10 numbers in order from least to greatest.

(Numbers will vary.)

6. READING AND COMPARING NUMBERS

STANDARD 6

Use the numeral cards (page 32) to show your phone number. Place it on the place-value chart (page 33) along with the phone numbers of the other members in your group. Take turns reading your phone numbers as whole numbers. Who has the phone number that forms the greatest number? The least number?

(Numbers will vary.)

7. USING CLUES AND A PLACE-VALUE CHART TO FIND A NUMBER

STANDARDS 6, 8

Use the numeral cards (page 32), the place-value chart (page 33), and these clues to find a mystery number:

a. The mystery number has 3 digits.
b. The digit in the ones place is 2 less than the digit in the tens place.
c. The digits in this mystery number add up to 5.
d. The digit in the hundreds place is the same as the digit in the ones place.

Write the number.

(The mystery number is 131.)

8. ADDING USING A PLACE-VALUE CHART

STANDARDS 6, 7, 13

Place each addend below on the place-value chart (page 33) using the numeral cards (page 32). Then, find each sum.

a. 2 + 4 = _?_
b. 12 + 4 = _?_
c. 32 + 4 = _?_
d. 102 + 4 = _?_
e. 2,582 + 4 = _?_

What pattern do you notice?

(a. 6; b. 16; c. 36; d. 106; e. 2,586. The digit in the ones place doesn't change.)

9. ESTIMATING NUMBER OF WORDS

STANDARDS 5, 8

Work with 2 or 3 other students to find about how many words there are on a page of the newspaper. Outline a small section of a page of newspaper that is mostly writing. Count each word in that section. Then estimate how many sections of the same size are on the page. Multiply the number of words in the sample section by the number of sections on the page.

Compare your group's findings with those of another group. Describe another way to estimate the number of words on a newspaper page.

(Estimates will vary. Other ways to estimate will vary, but may include: Count the number of

words in a line. Count the number of lines on the page. Multiply the two numbers.)

10. MONEY EQUIVALENCIES

STANDARDS 7, 8

Students at the Escalante Elementary School decided to save pennies to buy something special for the school. They saved 10,000 pennies! How many dollars is that? Explain your answer in writing or with an illustration.

($100. Answers may vary, but may include: Since there are 100 pennies in $1, divide 10,000 by 100. The answer is 100. Check students' drawings.)

11. NUMBERS OF YEARS

STANDARDS 2, 7, 8

Todd's Great-great-grandmother turns 100 years old today. About how many days has she lived? How many decades are there in 100 years? (Look *decade* up in a dictionary if you're not sure of its meaning.) What 1 word means *100 years*?

(About 36,500 days—100 x 365; there are 10 decades in 100 years; the word century means 100 years.)

12. ESTIMATING NUMBER OF BREATHS TAKEN

STANDARDS 2, 5, 7, 8

Have your partner time 1 minute while you count the number of breaths you take. Then switch roles. Estimate how many breaths you take in 1 day. About how many breaths do you take in 1 week? In 1 year? You may need to use a calculator to find the answers.

(Number of breaths taken in 1 minute will vary; estimates will vary. One possible answer, based on 20 breaths per minute: 20 x 60, or 1200 breaths each hour; 1200 x 24, or 28,800 breaths per day; 28,800 x 7, or 201,600 breaths per week; 201,600 x 52, or 10,483,200 breaths in a year.)

13. CALCULATING A SALARY

STANDARDS 4, 8

Suppose a basketball player just signed a contract for $100 million dollars, to be paid over the next 5 years.

  a. What will his salary be each year?
  b. About how much money is that each month? Each day? (You may need to use a calculator to solve this problem.)

What would you do if you received a salary like that?

(a. $20,000,000 per year; b. about $1,666,667 per month; about $55,556 per day. Answers will vary.)

14. MAP SKILLS

STANDARDS 4, 10

The Great Wall of China is over 2,000 miles long. Look on a map of the United States, and use the scale to find two cities about that same distance apart.

(Answers will vary, but may include: Boston, MA and Denver, CO or Savannah, GA and Las Vegas, NV.)

15. DISTANCES IN OUR SOLAR SYSTEM

STANDARDS 1, 4, 8, 10

Mercury is the closest planet to the sun. It is 58,000,000 kilometers away from the sun. Pluto, the farthest planet from the sun, is 5,900,000,000 kilometers away from it. How far apart are Mercury and Pluto?

(They are 5,842,000,000 kilometers apart.)

ACROSS THE CURRICULUM

Math Superlatives (Language Arts)

Have students bring in ads and clippings from newspapers and magazines that include words such as *the most, the biggest, the longest,* and so on. Have them identify what is being measured and what the measurement is. Discuss whether they think the claim is accurate.

Big Events (Language Arts)

Gather newspaper and magazine articles which use numbers in the thousands, billions, and beyond. Have children copy the numbers onto index cards. Students can put the cards in order from least to greatest number, practice reading the numbers, and match them with their corresponding articles.

Numeral Cards

0	0	0	1	1
1	2	2	2	3
3	3	4	4	4
5	5	5	6	6
6	7	7	7	8
8	8	9	9	9

Place-Value Chart

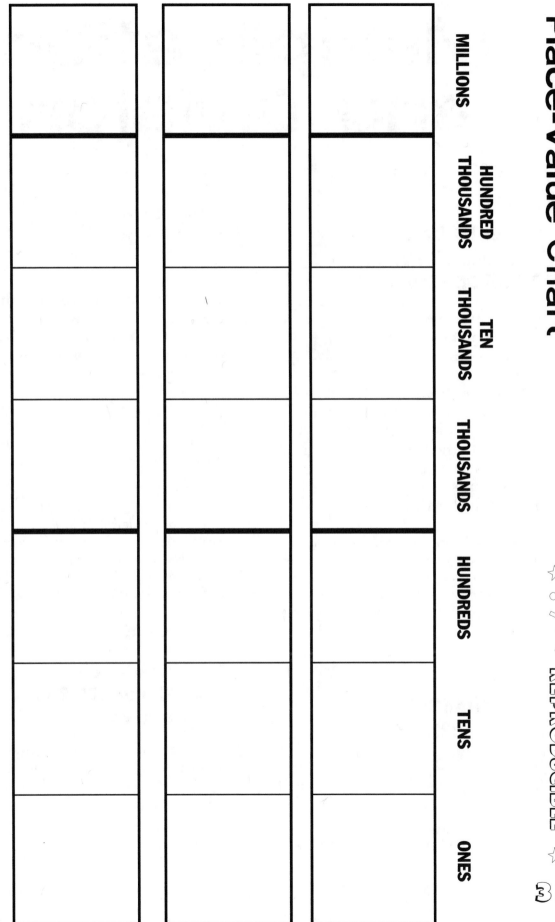

MILLIONS	HUNDRED THOUSANDS	TEN THOUSANDS	THOUSANDS	HUNDREDS	TENS	ONES

Multiplication and Division

1. IDENTIFYING MULTIPLICATION AND DIVISION SITUATIONS

STANDARDS 2, 4, 7

Have small groups of students brainstorm situations in their daily lives where they use multiplication and division. Write the headings *Multiplication* and *Division* on the board and record the examples given by each group as the students share the results of their brainstorming session.

(Examples will vary. Some possible examples: They may use division to determine the number of players to put on each team when playing a game; they may use multiplication to determine the price of 3 pencils when they know the price of 1 pencil.)

2a. RECTANGLES FOR THE NUMBER 6

STANDARDS 7, 8, 9

Look at the rectangle marked Figure 1 (page 43). The rectangle is formed by 1 square across and 6 squares down, so we can write 1 x 6 = 6 to describe

it. Turn the rectangle so it is 6 squares across and 1 square down. How does the multiplication sentence change?

Cut the squares apart. Rearrange them to form as many other rectangles for the number 6 as you can. Write a multiplication sentence for each one.

Take away one of the squares and arrange the 5 squares that are left into rectangles for the number 5. How many rectangles can you make?

(When the rectangle is turned it becomes a 6 by 1 rectangle, described by the multiplication sentence 6 x 1 = 6. The squares can be rearranged to show rectangles representing 2 x 3 = 6 and 3 x 2 =6. Two rectangles can be made with 5 squares—5 x 1 and 1 x 5.)

2b. RECTANGLES FOR THE NUMBER 24

STANDARDS 7, 8, 9

Write the multiplication sentence that describes the rectangle in Figure 2 (page 43). (First write the number of squares across, then write the number of squares down.)

Cut out the rectangle and cut apart

the squares. Rearrange them to form as many different rectangles for the number 24 as you can. Write a multiplication sentence for each one.

Take some squares away and experiment with making rectangles for lesser numbers. Find a number for which you can make 6 rectangles; 5 rectangles.

(4 x 6 = 24; 8 different rectangles can be made from the 24 squares. The multiplication sentences representing them are: 1 x 24 = 24, 24 x 1 = 24, 2 x 12 = 24, 12 x 2 = 24, 3 x 8 = 24, 8 x 3 = 24, 4 x 6 = 24, 6 x 4 = 24; 20, 18, and 12 can each be represented by 6 different rectangles. 16 can be represented by 5 rectangles.)

2c. IDENTIFYING PRIME NUMBERS

STANDARDS 3, 7, 8

You could make only 2 rectangles with 5 squares, a 1 x 5 rectangle and a 5 x 1 rectangle. The number 5 is a prime number. Each prime number has only two factors, itself and 1. Make a list of all the prime numbers between 1 and 25. You can use the squares from Figure 2 (page 43) to help.

(Prime numbers between 1 and 25: 2, 3, 5, 7, 11, 13, 17, 19, and 23.)

3. IDENTIFYING SQUARE NUMBERS

STANDARDS 7, 8, 9, 13

If you had 25 squares, you could make 1 large square (5 squares x 5 squares). The number 25 is a **square number.** Use the squares from the rectangle in Figure 2 (page 43) to find the number between 12 and 20 that is a square number. Write a multiplication sentence to describe the large square you made.

Find two square numbers that are less than 10. Write a multiplication sentence for each one. What do you notice about the multiplication sentences you wrote for the square numbers?

(The number 16—4 x 4 = 16; The numbers 4—2 x 2 = 4 and 9—3 x 3 = 9; Students should notice that the 2 factors in each multiplication sentence are the same.)

4. SQUARE NUMBERS BETWEEN 1 AND 144

STANDARDS 8, 13

Use the Product and Quotient Chart (page 44). Color in the product you get when you multiply each number from 1 to 12 by itself. For example, 1 x 1 = 1, color in the number 1 in the 1 column; 2 x 2 = 4, color in the number 4 in the 2 column, and so on. Remember, when 2 factors are the same number, the product is a square number. What pattern do you see when you color in the square numbers in the chart?

(The square numbers are in a diagonal line from the top left of the chart to the bottom right.)

5. FINDING PATTERNS OF MULTIPLES

STANDARDS 7, 13

Choose a number from the first column on the Product and Quotient Chart (page 44). Color in all the multiples of that number you find in the chart. For example, if you choose the number 7 from the first column, you would color in the numbers 7, 14, 21, and so on, wherever they appear in the chart. Write a sentence about the pattern you see.

(There are many different patterns for students to find—for example, multiples of 2 make a criss-cross pattern on the chart.)

6. USING MENTAL MATH TO FIND A PRODUCT

STANDARD 8

The Trojaks used 5 rolls of film taking pictures on their family vacation. Each roll of film had 24 pictures on it. Mrs. Trojak wants to know how many photos that will be in all. She doesn't have pencil and paper or a calculator. What mental math strategy could she use to find the product?

Make up a problem similar to this

one. Tell how you would solve it using mental math.

(Answers will vary. One possible answer: Think of 24 as 20 + 4, multiply 20 x 5 and 5 x 4 and add the products—100 + 20 = 120. The answer is 120 pictures. Problems and solutions will vary.)

7a. EXPLORING THE EFFECTS OF DOUBLING AMOUNTS

STANDARDS 3, 6, 7, 8

Suppose you were willing to take just 1 penny as allowance this week, as long as each week following, the amount would double. For example, this week you would get 1¢, next week 2¢, the following week 4¢, and so on. Do you think you'd be getting more than $10 or less than $10 for your allowance by the twelfth week?

Make a table to show what your allowance would be each week for 12 weeks. How much allowance would you receive the twelfth week? Is the amount greater or less than you thought it would be? How much allowance would you have received in all?

(Answers will vary. Allowance would be as follows:

Week 1 = 1¢	*Week 7 = 64¢*
Week 2 = 2¢	*Week 8 = $1.28*
Week 3 = 4¢	*Week 9 = $2.56*
Week 4 = 8¢	*Week 10 = $5.12*
Week 5 = 16¢	*Week 11 = $10.24*
Week 6 = 32¢	*Week 12 = $20.48*

You would receive $20.48 the twelfth week; Answers may vary, but most likely this amount is greater than the students thought it would be; total allowance received—$40.95.)

(105 times per week; 120 times per month; 1440 times per year. Comparisons will vary; numbers of times in a week, month, and year will vary.)

7b. EXPLORING MORE EFFECTS OF DOUBLING AMOUNTS

STANDARD 8

Suppose your allowance was $3.00 a week. How much allowance would you receive in 12 weeks? How does the total amount of allowance you receive compare with the total amount of allowance in problem 7a?

($36.00; the amount is less than the amount in problem 7a, which was $40.95.)

8. COMPARING SMILE STATISTICS

STANDARDS 4, 11

The average person smiles about 15 times a day. How many times would that be in a week? A month? A year? Keep a tally to count the number of times you smile in one day. How does the number compare with the average number?

If you smile about the same number of times each day, about how many times would that be in a week? A month? A year?

9. SOLVING A MULTI-STEP PROBLEM

STANDARDS 7, 8

"Ooh," moaned Ms. Martinez, "I have *so many* papers to grade!" Each child in her class had turned in 15 worksheets (except for 2 children who were absent). There are 29 children in her class. How many essays does Ms. Martinez have to grade?

Work with a partner to write out the steps you take to solve this problem. Find another way to solve the problem by changing the order of the steps.

(Ms. Martinez has 405 essays to correct; subtraction and multiplication are required to solve the problem, in either order. The subtraction can be done first and then the multiplication: 29 children - 2 absent children = 27 children, 27 children x 15 papers = 405 papers; or, the multiplication can be done first, and then the subtraction: 29 children x 15 papers = 435 papers, 2 absent children x 15 papers = 30 papers, 435 - 30 = 405 papers.)

10. SOLVING A MULTI-STEP PROBLEM

STANDARDS 1, 7, 8, 13

Work with a partner. Mrs. Lee decided that each member of her family should eat 3 fresh fruits and 2 fresh vegetables each day. There are 4 people in her family. She will buy apples, oranges, bananas, carrots, and potatoes this week. How many of each does she need to buy? How many fruits and vegetables is that in all? Tell what strategy you used to solve the problem.

(She needs to buy 28 of each fruit and vegetable; a total of 28 x 5, or 140 in all. Strategies may vary. Students may find it helpful to make a chart.)

Food Item	# Needed Each Day	# Needed For Week
carrots	4	28
potatoes	4	28
apples	4	28
oranges	4	28
bananas	4	28
TOTAL	20	140

11. COMPARING ESTIMATED AND ACTUAL PRODUCTS

STANDARDS 5, 7, 8

a. Describe a way to multiply 80 x 20 using mental math.

b. Round each factor to the nearest 10 and estimate the product for each of the following:

49 x 25   88 x 69   57 x 66

c. Is each estimate greater than or less than the actual product? How do you know?

(a. One possible strategy: Take off the 2 zeros and multiply—8 x 2 = 16. Add the 2 zeros back to make 1,600. b. 50 x 30 = 1,500; 90 x 70 = 6,300; 60 x 70 = 4,200; c. greater than; students should realize they rounded each factor up, so each estimate is greater than the actual product.)

12. DRAW A PICTURE TO SOLVE A MULTIPLICATION PROBLEM

STANDARDS 2, 4, 8

Draw a picture to solve this problem:
On a street there are 4 houses. In each house there are 6 rooms. In  each room are 5 pieces of furniture. How many rooms did you draw? How many pieces of furniture? Compare your drawing with a friend's.

(24 rooms—4 x 6 = 24; 120 pieces of furniture—24 x 5 = 120.)

ACROSS THE CURRICULUM

Favorite Recipes (Nutrition)

Ask children to bring in their favorite healthy-snack recipes. Children can work in small groups to increase or decrease the amounts of the ingredients in the recipes so that each recipe would make enough for the number of students in the class. Have children vote to select 1 or 2 recipes to make, and have children bring in the necessary ingredients. Enjoy the results!

13. DRAW A PICTURE TO SOLVE A MEASUREMENT PROBLEM

STANDARDS 1, 8, 9, 10

Amanda has a piece of paper 21 inches wide and 18 inches long. She wants to make a calendar. How many columns does she need? Most calendars have 5 rows, plus 1 more row for the names of the days of the week, making 6 rows. Amanda wants to make the columns and rows as large as possible. Draw a picture of the finished calendar, and label the length and width of 1 column and 1 row. What is the length and width of each box on the calendar?

(7 columns, one for each day of the week; picture should show a calendar divided into 7 columns and 6 rows. One column should be labeled 18 in. long and 3 in. wide; 1 row should be labeled 21 in. long and 3 in. wide; each box is 3 in. long and 3 in. wide.)

14. DIVISION WITH A FRACTION REMAINDER

STANDARDS 1, 8, 12

Matt was proud of catching 7 fish on a camping trip. The 4 other members of his family all wanted some fish when they smelled it cooking over the campfire. How can Matt divide the fish so everyone gets an equal share? How much will each person get?

(One possible answer: Each of the 5 family members gets 1 whole fish. The 2 remaining

fish are each divided into 5 pieces, with each person receiving 1/5 of both fish. So, each person gets a total of 1 2/5 fish.)

15. CREATING A PATTERN

STANDARDS 2, 8, 13

Kenisha plans to make 5 beaded bracelets to give as gifts. She buys 50 white beads, 25 blue beads, and 25 red beads. She will use the same number of each color bead for each bracelet. How many white beads will she use in one bracelet? Blue beads? Red beads?

Draw or write a pattern to show how Kenisha could string together the beads in one bracelet.

(10 white beads, 5 blue beads, 5 red beads; patterns will vary. One possible pattern: red-white-blue-white.)

16. WORKING WITH REMAINDERS

STANDARDS 1, 4, 8

Three classes of fifth graders and their 3 teachers are going on a field trip. Each group of 5 students needs an adult with them. They will invite some parent helpers to go on the trip. Permission slips have been returned by 92 students. Each bus seats 40 people. Work with 1 or 2 other students to determine:

a. how many adults are needed.
b. how many parent helpers should be invited.

c. how many buses will be needed.

(a. 92 ÷ 5 = 18 r2, so 19 adults are needed; b. there are already 3 teachers in the group, so 19 - 3, or 16 parent helpers should be invited; c. the total number of people going is 92 + 3 + 16, or 111. One bus seats 40 people, 2 buses seat 80 people, 3 buses seat 120 people, so 3 buses will be needed.)

17. DETERMINING THE BEST BUY

STANDARDS 3, 4, 5, 8

Tran was comparing different brands of colored pencils. He saw 1 set of 8 pencils for $1.99, another set of 12 pencils for $2.69, and a third set of 10 pencils for $2.39. About how much does each pencil cost in the 8-pencil set? The 12-pencil set? The 10-pencil set? Which set is the best buy? How did you get your answer? What are some things other than price to consider when choosing which colored pencil set to buy?

(8-pencil set—about 25¢ each, 12-pencil set—about 22¢ each, 10-pencil set—about 24¢ each. The set with the 12 colored pencils is the best buy. Strategies may vary but the best way may be to divide the price for each set by the number of pencils per set in order to find the cost of one pencil. Other things to consider may vary, but may include: the quality and size of the colored pencils in each set, the number of pencils you need, the amount of money you have with you.)

18. MULTIPLYING INGREDIENTS IN A RECIPE

STANDARDS 4, 8, 13

Molly gathered the ingredients she needed to make her famous breakfast sandwich. She got 1 egg, 1 slice of cheese, half a piece of ham, 2 slices of tomato, and 2 pieces of bread. Then her sister and brother asked her to fix each of them a breakfast sandwich. How much of each ingredient does Molly need to make three breakfast sandwiches?

(Molly needs 3 eggs, 3 slices of cheese, 1 1/2 pieces of ham, 6 tomato slices and 6 pieces of bread.)

19. DETERMINING QUANTITY AND COST

STANDARDS 3, 4, 8

The children at a day-care center like fruit freezes for a snack. The freezes come in packages of 12. Each package costs $0.89. There are 234 children at the day-care center. How many packages does the day-care center need to buy so that each child gets 1 freeze? How much will it cost to buy that many packages? Do the freezes cost more or less than 10¢ each?

(234 ÷ 12 = 19 r6, so the center needs to buy 20 packages to have enough for each child to get 1 freeze. It will cost 20 x $0.89, or $17.80. Each freeze costs less than 10¢ each—12 x 10¢ is $1.20, and each package costs only $0.89.)

20. MULTIPLYING 2-DIGIT NUMBERS

STANDARDS 2, 4, 8

In 1893, the original Ferris wheel was built for the World's Fair in Chicago. It was huge! There were 36 cars spaced around the wheel, and each car held 50 people. Draw a picture of the Ferris wheel. What is the greatest number of people that could ride on the Ferris wheel at one time? Do modern-day Ferris wheels carry more or fewer people than the original Ferris wheel?

(36 x 50, or 1,800 people. Modern-day Ferris wheels carry fewer people.)

21. NUMBERS DIVISIBLE BY 2

STANDARDS 6, 7, 8

Write the numbers from 15 to 30. Divide each one by 2. Copy and complete this sentence:

Numbers that can be divided by 2 with no remainder are all _____ numbers.

(15 ÷ 2 = 7 r1, 16 ÷ 2 = 8, 17 ÷ 2 = 8 r1, 18 ÷ 2 = 9, 19 ÷ 2 = 9 r1, 20 ÷ 2 = 10, 21 ÷ 2 = 10 r1, 22 ÷ 2 = 11, 23 ÷ 2 = 11 r1, 24 ÷ 2 = 12, 25 ÷ 2 = 12 r1, 26 ÷ 2 = 13, 27 ÷ 2 = 13 r1, 28 ÷ 2 = 14, 29 ÷ 2 = 14 r1, 30 ÷ 2 = 15; numbers that can be divided by 2 with no remainder are all even numbers.)

A C R O S S   T H E   C U R R I C U L U M

Old Time Journey (Social Studies)

When cars were first invented, in the early 1900's, the top speed for most automobiles was about 25 miles per hour. Children can research what it must have been like on a car trip in the early 20th century. About how long would a 100-mile drive have taken in 1900? What are some things that might have slowed down the traveler on that journey?

(A 100-mile drive would have taken at least 4 hours. Things that might have slowed the traveler down may vary, but may include: tires went flat quite often; there were no paved roads, gravel and dirt roads often had terrible potholes; there were places that were nearly impassable, such as swollen streams and eroded banks.)

22. NUMBERS DIVISIBLE BY 3

If a number is divisible by 3, it can be divided by 3 and there will be no remainder. Here is a way to check if a number is divisible by 3:

a. Add up all the digits.
b. If the sum is a number that is divisible by 3, then the original number is divisible by 3.

Copy the chart below and complete it, writing 4 numbers of your own that are divisible by 3.

#	Sum of Digits	Divisible by 3?	Check
54	5 + 4 = 9	yes	54 ÷ 3 = 18
132	1 + 3 + 2 = 6	yes	132 ÷ 3 = 44
516	5 + 1 + 6 = 12	yes	516 ÷ 3 = 172

(Numbers written in chart will vary.)

23. NUMBERS DIVISIBLE BY 4

Roberto says that if the last 2 digits of a number form a number divisible by 4, then the number itself is divisible by 4. He used 732 as an example:

"The last 2 digits of 732 are 32; 32 is divisible by 4, so 732 is divisible by 4. 732 divided by 4 is 183."

Write 10 numbers in which the last 2 digits make a number divisible by 4. See if Roberto's rule works each time.

(Numbers will vary. The rule will work each time.)

24. NUMBERS DIVISIBLE BY 5

The numbers 5, 10, 15, and 20 are **multiples** of 5. Write the next 10 multiples of 5. What pattern do you notice?

Every number that is a multiple of 5 is also divisible by 5. Write a rule to describe how to tell if a number is divisible by 5.

(25, 30, 35, 40, 45, 50, 55, 60, 65, 70; the last digit in each number is either zero or 5; if the last digit of a number is zero or 5, it is divisible by 5.)

25. NUMBERS DIVISIBLE BY 9

The numbers 36, 45, 54, 63, 72, 81, 90, 99, and 108 are all divisible by 9. Write 6 more numbers that are divisible by 9. Look at the numbers. Write a rule for identifying when a number is divisible by 9. (Hint: You may need to use a calculator to solve this problem.) Compare your rule with another pair's rule.

(Examples of numbers divisible by 9 may vary, but may include: 117, 126, 135, 144, 153, 162. The rule should include the idea that if the sum of all the digits is divisible by 9, the number is divisible by 9.)

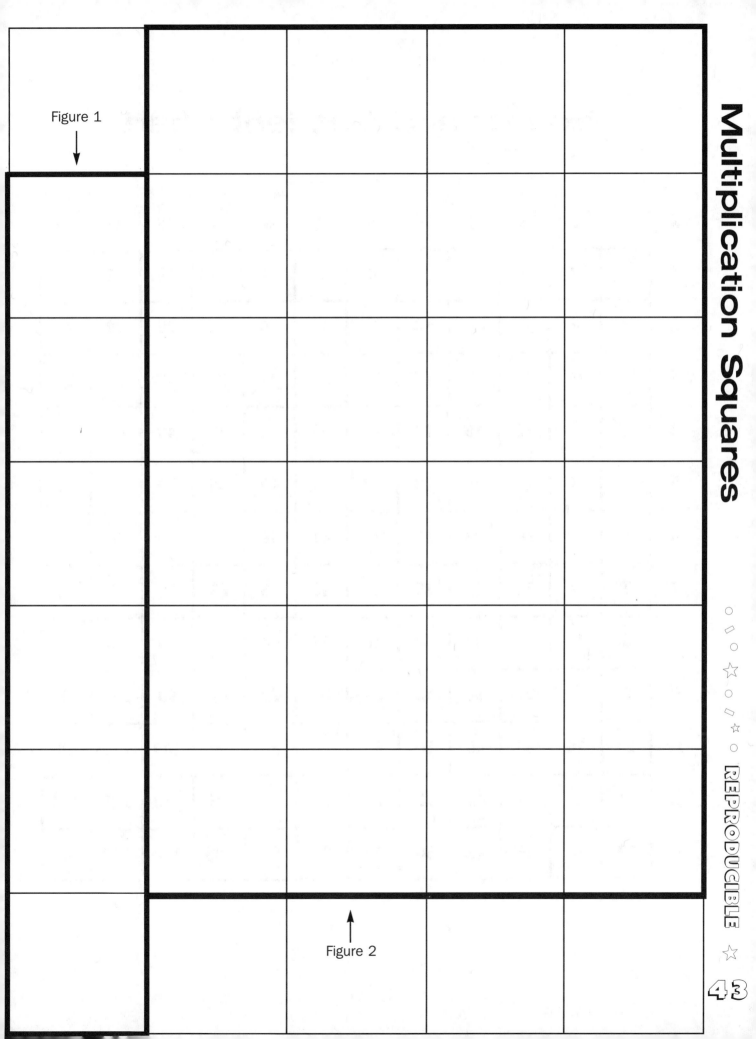

Figure 1

Figure 2

Product and Quotient Chart

X	1	2	3	4	5	6	7	8	9	10	11	12
1	1	2	3	4	5	6	7	8	9	10	11	12
2	2	4	6	8	10	12	14	16	18	20	22	24
3	3	6	9	12	15	18	21	24	27	30	33	36
4	4	8	12	16	20	24	28	32	36	40	44	48
5	5	10	15	20	25	30	35	40	45	50	55	60
6	6	12	18	24	30	36	42	48	54	60	66	72
7	7	14	21	28	35	42	49	56	63	70	77	84
8	8	16	24	32	40	48	56	64	72	80	88	96
9	9	18	27	36	45	54	63	72	81	90	99	108
10	10	20	30	40	50	60	70	80	90	100	110	120
11	11	22	33	44	55	66	77	88	99	110	121	132
12	12	24	36	48	60	72	84	96	108	120	132	144

Patterns and Codes

1. DRAWING AND EXTENDING A PATTERN

STANDARDS 9, 13

Draw 9 triangles. Color:

a. the second and sixth triangles purple.
b. all the odd triangles yellow.
c. the fourth and eighth triangles red.

If the pattern continues, what color will the 10th triangle be? Draw it. Then continue the pattern for 3 more triangles.

(Check students' drawings. The color pattern is yellow-purple-yellow-red; The 10th triangle is purple; the additional three triangles are yellow, red, yellow.)

2. IDENTIFYING AND EXTENDING PATTERNS

STANDARDS 8, 13

a. Describe this pattern and write the next 3 numbers: 37, 35, 33, 31, _?_ , _?_ , _?_
b. Describe this pattern and write the next 3 numbers: 35, 38, 41, 44, 47, _?_ , _?_ , _?_

c. Combine the patterns in *a* and *b* to create a new pattern, following these steps:

1. Begin by writing the number 35.
2. Use the pattern in *a* to write the next number.
3. Use the pattern in *b* to write the next number.
4. Repeat, alternating between the *a* pattern and the *b* pattern.
5. What are the first 5 numbers in the new pattern?

(a. subtract 2; next 3 numbers—29, 27, 25; b. add 3; next 3 numbers—50, 53, 56; c. first 5 numbers—35, 33, 36, 34, 37.)

3. CREATING AND EXTENDING PATTERNS

STANDARDS 1, 8, 13

Create a number pattern of your own. It can be an addition or subtraction pattern, an odd or even number pattern, a pattern of numbers that have common digits, or any other pattern you can think of. Trade patterns with your partner. Describe the pattern and write the next 5 numbers.

(Patterns and numbers will vary.)

4. SHAPE, NUMBER, AND COLOR PATTERNS IN THE CLASSROOM

STANDARDS 2, 4, 9, 13

There are probably many shape, number, and color patterns in your classroom. For example, the ceiling tiles could have patterns of dots. That is a shape pattern. The calendar may show the numbers 7, 14, 21, 28 in one column. That is a number pattern. The bulletin board could have a blue and white border around it. That is a color pattern.

Work with your partner to find a shape, a number, and a color pattern in your classroom. Draw a picture or write a description of each one.

(Patterns and descriptions will vary.)

5. EXTENDING PATTERNS FROM VERBAL MEMORY

STANDARDS 2, 9, 13

Look at the shape pattern in Figure 1 (page 52) for 30 seconds. Turn the page over so you can't see the shapes and describe the pattern to yourself. Look at the pattern again for 10 seconds, then again turn the paper over. From memory, draw the next 3 shapes in the pattern. Compare your drawing to Figure 1.

(Children's drawings should show 3 shapes the same as the first 3 shapes in Figure 1, page 52.)

6. EXTENDING PATTERNS FROM MEMORY

STANDARDS 2, 9, 13

Look at the shape pattern in Figure 2 (page 52) for 30 seconds. Turn the page over so you can't see the shapes. Close your eyes and try to picture the pattern in your mind. Look at the pattern again for 10 seconds, then again turn the paper over. From memory, draw the next row in the pattern. Compare your drawing to Figure 2.

(Children's drawings should show a row of shapes identical to each row in Figure 2, page 52.)

7. DRAWING AND EXTENDING A PATTERN

STANDARDS 2, 9, 13

Cut out the shapes in Figures 1 and 2 (page 52). Take turns with your partner mixing up the shapes and arranging them to create a new pattern. Have your partner describe the pattern you have created. Draw each pattern you make.

(Patterns shown in drawings will vary.)

ACROSS THE CURRICULUM

Patterns in Poetry (Language Arts)

Poems often have sound patterns created by rhyme and rhythm. Write a simple poem such as the following on the board:

Jack and Jill went up a hill
To fetch a pail of water.
Jack fell down and broke his crown,
And Jill came tumbling after.

Have students read the poem aloud and identify the pairs of rhyming words (Jill, hill; down, crown; water, after). Have them read the poem again, clapping softly to identify the rhythm in each line.

Have students work in pairs. Ask each pair to write a short poem. Have pairs read their poems and have other students identify the rhyme and rhythm patterns.

8. PRESIDENTIAL-ELECTION YEAR PATTERN

STANDARDS 4, 8, 13

Every 4 years we have presidential elections. The first election of the 21st century is in November, 2000. Between 2000 and 2025, which years will be presidential election years? What issues do you think people will be concerned with in 2025?

(2004, 2008, 2012, 2016, 2020, 2024; issues will vary but may include: the economy, technology, the environment, space exploration.)

9. FINDING A PATTERN TO SOLVE A PROBLEM

STANDARDS 8, 13

Jake and Jody went on a camping trip. On Monday, they saw some tents near their campsite. On Tuesday, they saw twice as many tents as the day before, and on Wednesday, 3 times as many tents as on Monday. On Thursday, they saw 8 tents—2 more than on Wednesday. Friday, they saw 2 more tents than on Thursday, which was 5 times as many as on Monday.

Make a table. Describe the pattern you see. How many tents did they see on Monday? If the pattern continues, how many tents will they see on Saturday?

Day of the Week	M	T	W	TH	F
Number of Tents	2	4	6	8	10

(The number of tents increases by 2 each day; they saw 2 tents on Monday; they will see 12 tents on Saturday.)

10. SOUND AND MOVEMENT PATTERNS

STANDARDS 4, 13

Rhythm is very important to dancers and musicians. Rhythm is conveyed in the pattern of sounds in music and the pattern of movement in dance. Have students work together in small groups to create a rhythm using sound (by tapping, clapping, or stamping) or a rhythm using movement. Have each group demonstrate their sound or movement pattern and teach it to the rest of the class.

(Rhythms created will vary.)

11. FIBONACCI SEQUENCE

STANDARDS 4, 8, 13

There is a special pattern of numbers called the **Fibonacci sequence,** named after the man who discovered it. He studied the natural world and noticed a pattern in the numbers of things, such as petals on flowers and leaves on stems. This is how the Fibonacci sequence begins:
1, 1, 2, 3, 5, 8, 13, 21, 34

Describe the pattern. Discuss it with your partner. Predict what the next number in the sequence is.

(Each number in the sequence is the sum of the 2 numbers before it. Predictions will vary. The next number is 55.)

12. FINDING EXAMPLES OF THE FIBONACCI NUMBERS

STANDARDS 2, 4, 8, 13

Have students take a walk around the outside of the school and look for things in nature that represent one or more numbers of the Fibonacci sequence — 1, 2, 3, 5, 8, 13, 21, 34, 55, 89, and so on. For example, the number of petals on a flower may be 5 or 8. The leaves on a stem might be clustered in groups of 5. Have students record what they find on the walk. Back in the classroom, make a class list of the items found and the Fibonacci numbers they represent.

(Answers will vary.)

13. ILLUSTRATING NUMBERS FROM THE FIBONACCI SEQUENCE

STANDARDS 2, 4, 13

Draw a picture of something from nature that represents numbers from the Fibonacci Sequence. For example, a stem with 2 leaves on the left side, then 3 leaves on the right, then 2 leaves on the left, and 1 on the right. On the stem is a flower with 13 petals.

(Answers will vary.)

Musical Patterns (Music)
Explain that manufactured objects also often exhibit Fibonacci proportions. Use piano keys as an example (although there are 88 instead of 89 keys): there are clusters of 2 black keys above 3 white keys and 3 black keys above 5 white keys; octaves are made up of 8 keys.

Invite the music teacher or a volunteer musician to demonstrate and discuss patterns in music with students.

14a. VALUES OF ROMAN NUMERALS

STANDARDS 6, 8, 13

Use the Roman Numeral Chart in Figure 1 (page 53) to decipher the value of the following numerals:

CLXV, MCMXCIX, DXXXII.

(165, 1999, 532)

14b. USING ROMAN NUMERALS

STANDARDS 6, 8, 13

Use the Roman Numeral Chart in Figure 1 (page 53) to rewrite the following street address and phone number using numerals from our number system (1, 2, 3, and so on):

address: CLX Payson Rd.
phone :   IX II VI - VIII VII IV I

Write your street address and phone number using Roman numerals. (Think of your phone number as seven separate digits.)

Switch papers with your partner and rewrite his or her address and phone number using numbers from our number system.

(160 Payson Rd.; 926-8741; addresses and phone numbers will vary.)

15. HINDU NUMERALS

STANDARDS 2, 3, 4, 13

The people who invented our number system lived in India about 2,000 years ago. The system they used is called the Hindu system. The Arabs developed the system further and eventually the symbols evolved into the numerals we use today.

Look at the Hindu numeral chart in Figure 2 (page 53). Write the date you were born (month, day, year) using the Hindu numerals.

(Birth dates will vary.)

16. PICTOGRAPHS

STANDARDS 2, 4, 13

Native Americans drew pictographs to tell stories, describe events, or record information. Pictographs used symbols for animals, people, and objects. Without using a symbol for the number 4, how could you represent 4 deer in a pictograph?

Write a sentence about yourself or your family that includes a number, for example: "Our family has 3 guinea pigs." Draw a pictograph to represent your sentence. Trade papers with your partner and write the sentence shown by his or her pictograph.

(Draw 4 of the symbols used to represent a deer. Sentences and pictographs will vary.)

17. FINDING YOUR LUCKY NUMBER

STANDARDS 4, 8

Here's a way to find a number some people believe to be a lucky number:

- Write down your birth date using numbers (month, day, and year).

- Find the sum of all the digits. For example, 5/11/1988 would be $5 + 1 + 1 + 1 + 9 + 8 + 8 = 33$.

- Add the digits of the 2-digit number together. If the sum is a 2-digit number, add those digits together. Repeat until you get a 1-digit number. That's your lucky number!

Some people believe that a person's lucky number can tell about his or her personality. What do you think?

(Lucky numbers will vary; answers will vary.)

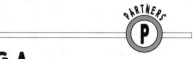

18. USING A NUMBER-LETTER CODE

STANDARDS 2, 4, 13

Follow these simple directions to turn words into number codes using the code wheel (p. 54): Cut the wheels out, poke a hole through each center, and place the smaller wheel on top of the larger one, lining up the holes. Put a brass paper fastener through the holes to keep the wheels together.

Turn your code wheel so the number 8 lines up with the letter A. To write the number code for the word *hat*, write the numbers that line up with the letters *H*, *A*, and *T*. What is the number code for *hat*?

Keep the number 8 lined up with the letter A on your code wheel. Write a sentence. Write the number code for each word in the sentence. Trade coded sentences with your partner. Decode your partner's sentence.

(The number code for hat is 15–8–1; sentences will vary.)

19. USING A NUMBER-LETTER CODE

STANDARDS 2, 4, 13

Follow the directions in number 18 (page 50) to construct a code wheel (page 54). Then decode this sentence. (Hint: 23–7 is the number code for the word *is.*)

8–3–18–15–13   23–7   13–3–9–6
26–9–17–25–13   18–15–13.

(Today is your lucky day.)

20. CREATING A CODE

STANDARDS 1, 2, 4, 13

Assemble your code wheels (see the directions in number 18) to make up your own code. You can write numbers for letters, or you can use other symbols. Write a sentence using your code. Then write a key that describes how to decode it. Trade papers with your partner. Decode the sentence he or she wrote.

(Codes and sentences will vary.)

Ancient Stories (Social Studies)

Children can research how the ancient Romans, Hindus, or Native Americans lived. They can then write word problems incorporating the researched information and using the numerals and other symbols they learned about in this chapter.

Patterns

Figure 1

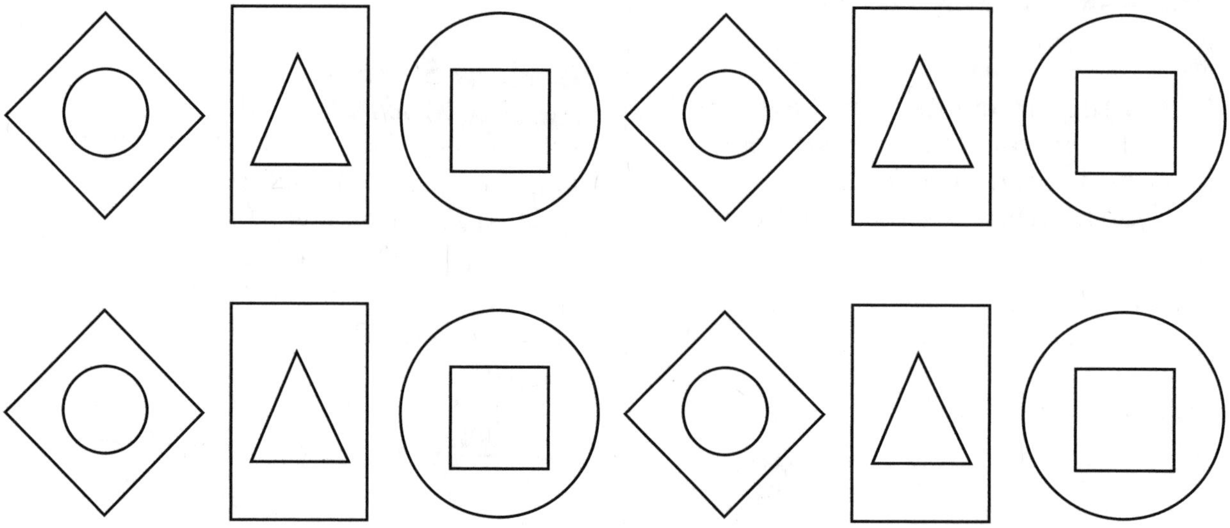

Figure 2

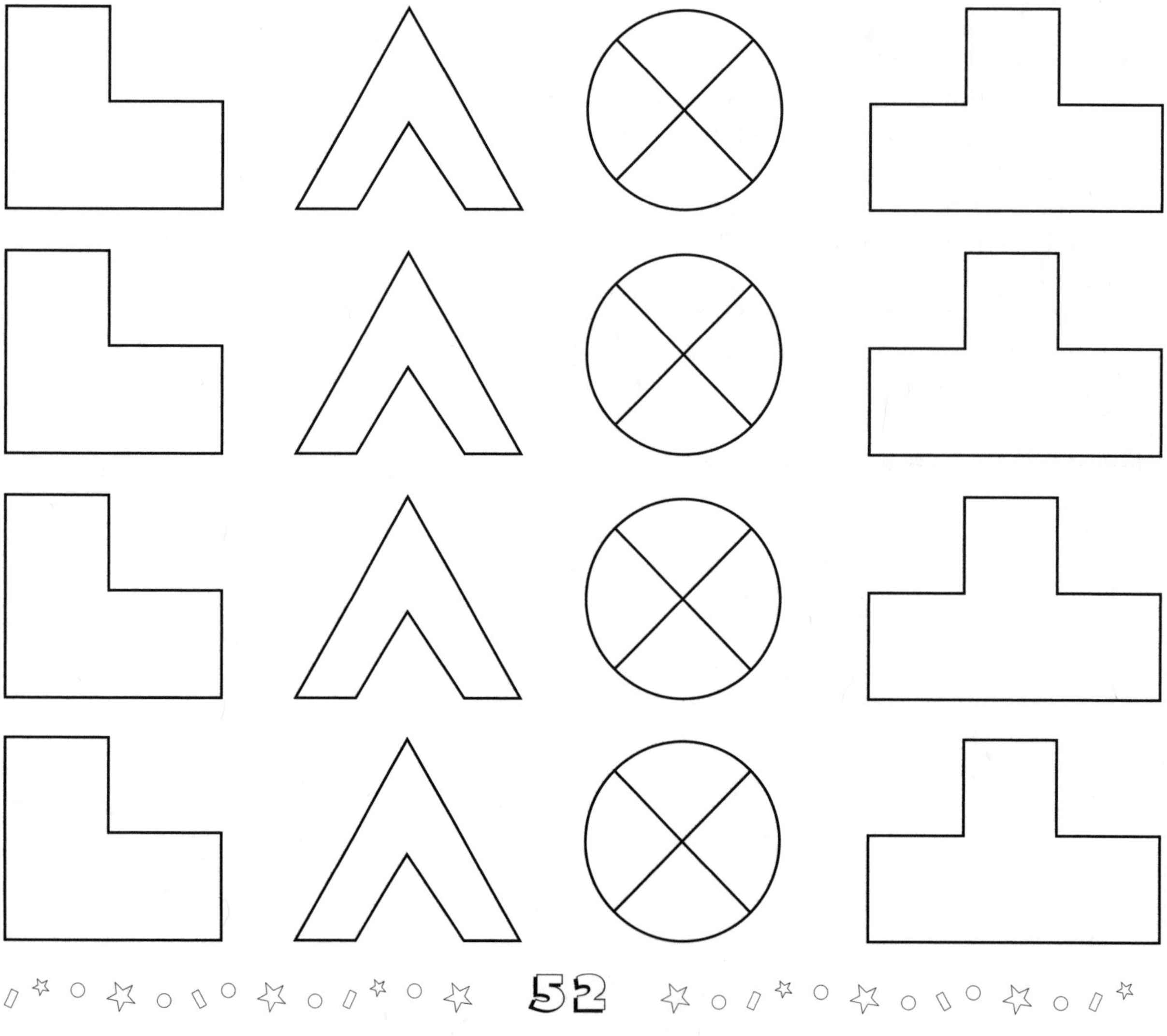

Ancient Numeration Systems

Figure 1

ROMAN NUMERALS			
1	I	9	IX
2	II	10	X
3	III	50	L
4	IV	100	C
5	V	500	D
6	VI	900	CM
7	VII	1000	M
8	VIII		

Figure 2

HINDU NUMERALS			
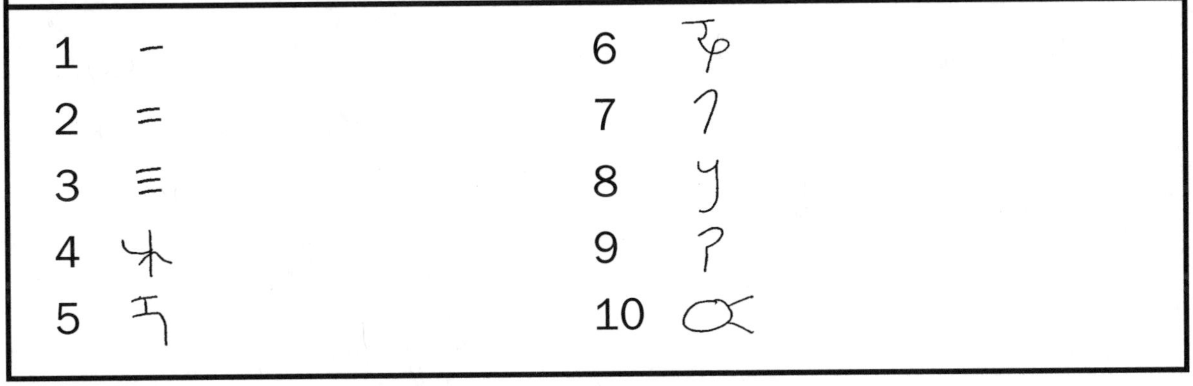 1	—	6	𝄢
2	=	7	フ
3	☰	8	Ƴ
4	𝖄	9	?
5	𝖅	10	⚮

Code Wheel

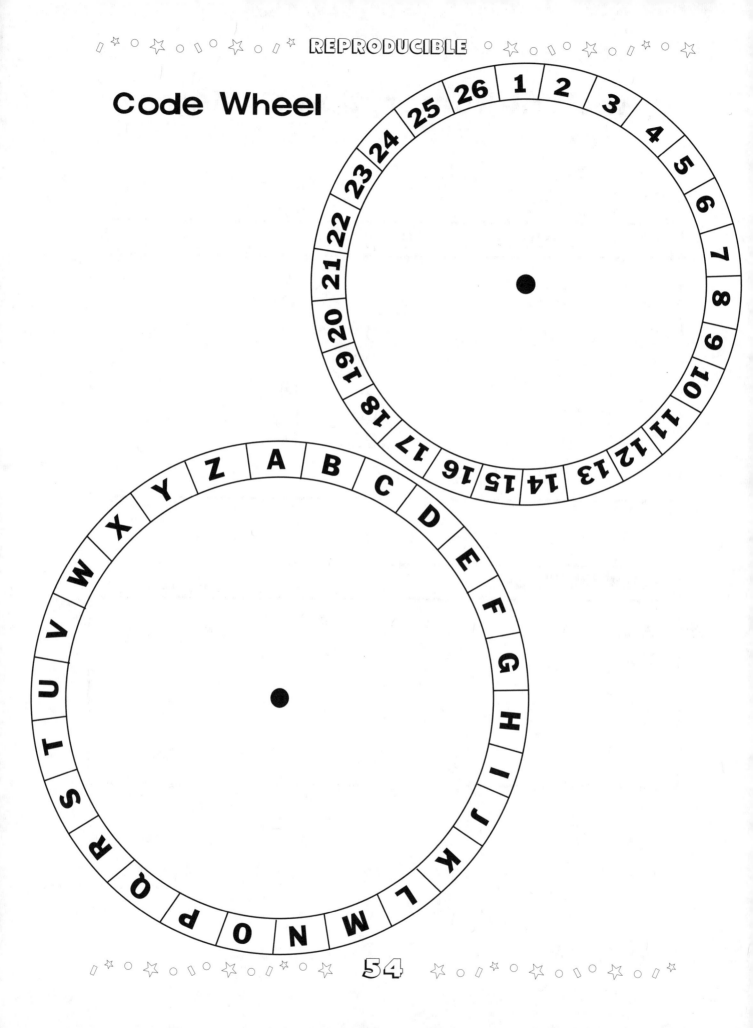

CHAPTER 6

Fractions, Decimals, and Percents

1. PAPER FOLDING– HALVES

STANDARDS 9, 12

Fold a sheet of paper in half. How many sections do you have when you unfold it? How many sections do you think you will have if you fold the paper in half, then in half again? And in half a third time? Fold the paper to check your predictions. Will the number of sections be the same with paper of any size and shape?

(2 sections; predictions will vary. A paper folded in half twice will have 4 sections. A paper folded in half 3 times will have 8 sections; Yes, the number of sections would be the same for any size and shape of paper.)

2. THINGS THAT CAN AND CAN'T BE DIVIDED IN HALF

STANDARDS 4, 12

List 3 things that would be just as good if you cut them in half. List 3 things that would be ruined if you cut them in half.

(Answers will vary, but may include: cookies, sandwiches, oranges; answers will vary, but may include: money, clothing, and books.)

3. APPLYING THE CONCEPT OF ONE THIRD

STANDARDS 2, 12

Draw a circle and divide it into 3 equal sections. Shade 1 section. 1/3 is the fraction that describes the shaded part. Tell a story that has the fraction 1/3 in it.

(Check children's circles; stories will vary.)

4. FRACTIONS EQUAL TO 1

STANDARDS 2, 12

Cut out each fraction strip (page 62). Then cut up each strip into equal sections, cutting along the dotted lines. You should have two 1/2 sections, three 1/3 sections, four 1/4 sections, and so on.

Cover up the strip representing 1 whole (labeled with 1) with 3 different combinations of fraction sections. Record the combinations by writing number sentences, for example, 1/2 + 1/4 + 1/8 + 1/8 = 1.

(Number sentences will vary, but may include: 1/2 + 1/3 + 1/6; 1/3 + 1/6 + 1/6 + 1/9 +

1/9 + 1/9; 1/2 + 1/4 + 1/12 + 1/12 + 1/12.)

5. COMPARING FRACTIONS

STANDARDS 6, 12

Cut out each fraction strip (page 62) to play the following fraction comparison game: One partner picks 2 sections. The other partner compares the sections and records the comparison using >, <, or =. Continue taking turns choosing fractions and comparing them in writing until both partners have recorded 5 comparisons.

(Recorded comparisons will vary.)

6. FINDING EQUIVALENT FRACTIONS

STANDARDS 2, 12

Cut out each fraction strip (page 62). Follow these steps to find equivalent fractions:

a. One partner chooses a fraction section.
b. The other partner tries to find 2 or more fraction sections that when placed together are **equivalent,** or the same size as, the first fraction section.
c. If the partner finds 2 or more sections that are equivalent, he or she records it in a number sentence. For example, 1/8 + 1/16 + 1/16 = 1/4.

d. If the partner cannot find 2 or more sections that are equivalent, he or she records the fraction and writes, *No equivalent sections found.*
e. Continue taking turns choosing and finding equivalent sections until each partner has written 5 number sentences.

(Number sentences for equivalencies will vary. Students will not be able to find 2 or more sections equivalent to 1/5, 1/9, 1/12, or 1/16.)

7. FRACTION OF A NUMBER

STANDARDS 4, 12

Cyrus and his dad are making spaghetti for dinner. The recipe makes enough spaghetti for 12 people, but they only need to make enough for 1/4 that number. For how many people are they making spaghetti?

This is the ingredient list from the recipe:

4 cans tomato sauce
2 cans tomato paste
8 cups chopped tomatoes
4 pounds of spaghetti

Rewrite the ingredient list so Cyrus and his dad will make just the amount of spaghetti they need.

(3 people; 1 can tomato sauce, 1/2 can tomato paste, 2 cups chopped tomatoes, 1 pound spaghetti.)

8. ADDING FRACTIONS

STANDARDS 4, 12

Kiko has a little dog, Shadow, and Sophie has a very big dog, Rolly. Shadow eats 1/3 as much as Rolly. Rolly eats 1 bag of dog food each week. How much does Shadow eat each week? How much does Rolly eat in 8 weeks? How much does Shadow eat in 8 weeks? Work with your partner to make a table to find the answers.

(Shadow eats 1/3 of a bag of dog food in a week; Rolly will eat 8 bags of food in 8 weeks; Shadow will eat 2 2/3 bags of food in 8 weeks. One possible table:

Number of Bags of Dog Food Eaten

| Week | Dogs | |
	Rolly	Shadow
1	1	$1/3$
2	2	$2/3$
3	3	1
4	4	$1\frac{1}{3}$
5	5	$1\frac{2}{3}$
6	6	2
7	7	$2\frac{1}{3}$
8	8	$2\frac{2}{3}$

ACROSS THE CURRICULUM

Fraction Feast (Nutrition)

Ask children to bring in food items that can be cut into many equal pieces. Some possible items are fruits such as bananas and apples, brownies or anything else baked in a rectangular pan, tortillas, cheese, and, of course, pizza. Discuss the variety of the shapes and sizes of the food. As each food item is cut into equal pieces, discuss the fractions represented. For example, if an apple is cut into 6 wedges, one wedge represents 1/6 of the apple, 2 wedges 1/3 of the apple, and so on.

9. DIVIDING A LESSER NUMBER BY A GREATER NUMBER

STANDARDS 1, 2, 4, 12

Suppose you have 3 friends over to play, and everybody (including you) wants a snack. But there are only 3 cupcakes. Draw a picture to show how you will divide the cupcakes so each person gets an equal share.

(Drawings may vary but should show that each person would receive 3/4 of a cupcake.)

10. COMPARING NON-UNIT FRACTIONS

STANDARDS 6, 12

Use what you know about fractions to write these fractions in order from least to greatest: 4/5, 3/4, 7/8, 2/3.

Compare your answer with your partner's.

Describe 1 way you could check your answers.

(2/3, 3/4, 4/5, 7/8; ways to check answers will vary, but may include: Compare the fractions using the strips on page 62; Write an equivalent fraction for each using the lowest common denominator (12), and compare the numerators.)

11. FRACTIONS EQUAL TO 1

STANDARDS 2, 6, 12

Juan, Jaime, and Joel are brothers who were working together to paint a fence. Juan, who is the oldest, said he'd paint half the fence. Jaime, the middle brother, said he'd paint one third of the fence. Joel, the youngest, would paint whatever part was left. Draw a picture to show how much of the fence each brother painted. Then write a number sentence describing your picture.

(Drawings should show that Juan painted half of the fence, Jaime 1/3, and Joel 1/6; 1/2 + 1/3 + 1/6 = 1.)

12. A FRACTION OF A FRACTION

STANDARDS 2, 12

Draw a picture to show that 1/4 of 1/2 is the same as 1/2 of 1/4.

(Pictures may vary. One possible picture:

1/4 of 1/2

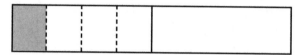

1/2 of 1/4

13. FINDING HALF OF A FRACTION

STANDARDS 1, 2, 12

Devon and Troy decide to combine their money to buy a pizza. Troy has only half as much money as Devon, so he is only going to eat half as much pizza. How much of the pizza will each one eat? Draw a picture to find the answer.

(Devon will eat 2/3 of the pizza, and Troy will eat 1/3; pictures will vary.)

14. RATIOS

STANDARDS 9, 12, 13

Make a design showing diamonds and triangles in a 1 to 4 ratio; that is, for every diamond you draw, draw 4 triangles. If you draw 2 diamonds, how many triangles should you draw?

Make another design with diamonds and triangles, but use a different ratio. Trade drawings with your partner and write the ratio it shows.

(8 triangles; designs will vary; ratios will vary.)

15. FINDING FRACTIONS IN THE WORLD AROUND US

STANDARDS 4, 12

Have groups of students brainstorm ways fractions are used inside the classroom and outside the classroom. Have groups share their findings and record them on a class list.

(Answers will vary but may include: telling time—half hour, quarter hour; measuring—quarter mile, half gallon; playing music—half notes, eighth notes.)

ACROSS THE CURRICULUM

Enlarging a Drawing (Art)

Have students use page 63 and enlarge the drawing of the make-believe creature using a 1:3 ratio. Explain that each part of the monster drawn on the small grid will be drawn 3 times larger on the big grid. Instruct them to draw what is in each square in the small grid in the corresponding square in the big grid, beginning with the square in the top left-hand corner.

16. PLACES WHERE DECIMALS ARE USED

STANDARDS 4, 12

Often decimals are used instead of fractions to show amounts less than 1, or amounts between whole numbers. Name 2 places where decimals are used, and give 3 examples of the decimals that may be used there.

(Answers will vary, but may include: at the deli counter in a grocery store—0.25 pounds, 1.5 pounds, 2.75 pounds; at athletic events—a time of 14.12 minutes, a batting average of 0.345.)

17. WRITING DECIMALS

STANDARDS 3, 6, 12

Tina used a spinner to get these digits: 5, 9, 2, 7, 4, 1. She is going to use the digits to write decimals. The only rule is she must have at least 1 digit on either side of the decimal point.

What is the greatest possible decimal Tina can write using all the digits? What is the least possible decimal Tina can write using all the digits?

(97542.1; 1.24579)

18. FINDING PERCENTS

STANDARDS 11, 12

If 20% of the people in a city drive red cars, what percentage of people in the city do not drive red cars?

Make up a question of your own that has an answer of 60%.

(80% of the people do not drive red cars; questions may vary, but should include a combination of numbers that add up to 100%.)

19. DRAWING TO SHOW PERCENTS

STANDARD 12

Circle the 4 squares made up of 100 smaller squares on the Fractions and Decimals page (page 64). Label each of these squares a, b, c, or d, and in each square draw one of the following:

a. a design, 30% of which is colored blue
b. the letter "L", so that it covers 14% of the square
c. a design, 25% of which is yellow and 75% of which is green
d. a house that covers 60% of the square.

(Check students' drawings.)

20. DRAWING TO SHOW EQUIVALENT FRACTIONS AND DECIMALS

STANDARDS 6, 12

Use the Fractions and Decimals reproducible (page 64). In the 2 squares in #1, color in 1/4 of the top square and 0.25 of the bottom square. What do you notice?

Color in the same amount in each pair of squares in the next 3 sections to show other equivalent fraction and decimal pairs. Write each equivalent fraction and decimal pair shown.

(The same amount of each square is colored; equivalent fraction and decimal pairs will vary.)

21. WRITING PERCENTS AND FRACTIONS AS DECIMALS

STANDARDS 4, 12

There is a lot of water in the food we eat. A water- melon is 98% water. A potato is 3/4 water. An apple is 4/5 water. Write these foods in order from the least amount of water to the greatest amount. (Remember, 3/4 means the same as 3 ÷ 4.) Compare your answer with your partner's. (If necessary, you may use a calculator to solve this problem.)

(From least amount of water to greatest: potato, apple, watermelon.)

22. ADDING AND MULTIPLYING DECIMALS

STANDARDS 4, 12

Bobby is earning money for a charity by doing a walk-a-thon. For every tenth of a mile he walks, he earns a quarter for the charity. The first hour he walked 2.3 miles. The sec- ond hour he walked 2.9 miles. The third hour he walked 3.1 miles, and the fourth hour he walked 1.8 miles. How many miles did he walk? How much money did he earn?

(10.1 miles; $25.25)

23. WRITING PERCENT PROBLEMS

STANDARDS 2, 6, 12

Make up a quiz on percents to give to your partner. Ask questions like the following: 5 is 50% of what num- ber?

The answer to the question is 10. Make up 5 questions in all. Trade quizzes. Correct the quizzes together.

(Questions will vary.)

Fraction Strips

1															

1/2	1/2

1/4	1/4	1/4	1/4

1/8	1/8	1/8	1/8	1/8	1/8	1/8	1/8

1/16	1/16	1/16	1/16	1/16	1/16	1/16	1/16	1/16	1/16	1/16	1/16	1/16	1/16	1/16	1/16

1/12	1/12	1/12	1/12	1/12	1/12	1/12	1/12	1/12	1/12	1/12	1/12

1/3	1/3	1/3

1/6	1/6	1/6	1/6	1/6	1/6

1/9	1/9	1/9	1/9	1/9	1/9	1/9	1/9	1/9

1/5	1/5	1/5	1/5	1/5

Enlarging a Drawing

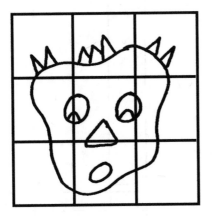

Fractions and Decimals

Section 1

Section 2

Section 3

Section 4

Geometry and Spatial Awareness

1. IDENTIFYING SHAPES AND ESTIMATING SIZES

STANDARDS 2, 5, 9, 10

Draw and label as many things as you can that are the same shape as a quarter. Estimate whether each one is smaller or larger than a quarter. Compare the items to a real quarter to check your estimates.

(Items and estimates will vary, but may include: the face of a watch [same size as quarter], the bottom of a pencil or marker [smaller], and the bottom of a paper cup [larger].)

2. ESTIMATING SIZE

STANDARDS 2, 5, 9, 10

Draw the following items from memory (no looking!), trying to make them actual size: paper clip, pen, ruler. Compare your drawings to the real items. How did you do in estimating the sizes?

(Comparisons will vary. Children should indicate whether the drawn objects were larger, smaller, or the same size as the actual items.)

3. IDENTIFYING RECTANGLES AND THEIR ATTRIBUTES

STANDARDS 4, 9

Make a list of everything you see, from where you are sitting, that has a rectangular shape. Describe 2 ways all rectangles are the same.

(Lists will vary. Descriptions of rectangles will vary but should include 2 of the following: 4 sides, 2 pairs of parallel sides, 4 right angles [or square corners].)

4. IDENTIFYING A SHAPE FROM ITS DESCRIPTION

STANDARDS 3, 9, 10

Look at the four-sided shapes in Figure 1 (page 73). Write the number of the shape that fits the following description:

Each of its corners is a square corner, or right angle.
Two of the sides are twice as long as the other 2 sides.

Draw 1 of the other 4-sided shapes from Figure 1 and write a description of it.

(#3; descriptions will vary, but may include: #1—each of its corners is a square corner, or right angle. All 4 sides are the same length; #2—its corners are not all the same size. All 4 sides are the same length; #4—its corners are not all the same size. Only 2 of the sides are the same length.)

5. DESCRIBING AND IDENTIFYING SHAPES

STANDARDS 2, 3, 9, 10

Take turns describing a shape in Figure 1 (page 73) for your partner to identify. Without mentioning the name of the shape, you can describe the sides as slanted or straight, the lengths of sides, or sizes of angles, and so on. Give only 1 clue at a time. See how many different ways you can describe each shape, and how few clues are needed to identify it.

(Answers will vary.)

6. DRAWING TRIANGLES

STANDARDS 2, 9, 10

Draw each triangle described below. Label each one with the same letter as its description—*a*, *b*, or *c*.
   a. None of the 3 sides are the same length.

b. Two of the 3 sides are the same length.
c. All 3 angles, or corners, are the same size.

(Drawings should show: a. a scalene triangle, b. an isosceles triangle, c. an equilateral triangle.)

7. VISUALIZATION • PAPER FOLDING AND CUTTING

STANDARDS 2, 3, 9

Suppose you folded a piece of paper in half and made 3 cuts along the fold, as shown in Figure 2 (page 73). What shapes do you think you would see when you unfolded the paper? Draw your prediction.

Now, fold and cut a piece of paper as shown. What shapes do you see when you unfold the paper? How do the results compare with your predictions?

(Predictions will vary. The top shape is a triangle, the middle shape is a rhombus, and the bottom shape is an oval.)

8. VISUALIZATION • PAPER FOLDING AND CUTTING

STANDARDS 2, 3, 9

Take a piece of paper and fold it in half. Make some cuts along the fold. Predict, in writing or drawing, what the paper will look like when you unfold it. Unfold the paper to check your prediction.

Repeat the activity, this time folding a piece of paper in half twice.

Write a few sentences describing how the unfolded papers compared with your predictions.

(Predictions and sentences will vary.)

ACROSS THE CURRICULUM

Shape Poetry: (Language Arts)
Have children write poems describing objects. Model how to arrange the words of the poem into the shape of the object using the example given below. Display the poems for everyone to enjoy.

all
diamonds shimmer
their light is reflected into
a thousand points of
color

9. PAPER FOLDING · SIXTHS

STANDARD 3, 9, 10

Divide a sheet of paper into 6 equal sections by drawing 5 lines. Divide another sheet of paper into 6 equal sections by drawing only 3 lines.

(Answers may vary.)

10. PAPER FOLDING · CUBE

STANDARDS 3, 9

Look at the shape in Figure 1 on the Silhouette page (page 74). Think about how you could fold it into a cube. Test your idea by cutting out the shape and folding and taping it into a cube. Write or draw the steps you took to do it.

(Answers and drawings will vary.)

11. INTERSECTING, PERPENDICULAR, AND PARALLEL LINES

STANDARDS 2, 3, 9

Two lines on a plane (a 2-dimensional surface), can intersect or be parallel to one another. Some lines that intersect may be perpendicular to each other.

Use a ruler, a sheet of paper, and a red and green marker. Take turns drawing lines with your partner. Draw the lines going in different directions, from 1 edge of the paper to another edge.

Take turns drawing circles around points where lines intersect, outlining perpendicular lines in red, and outlining parallel lines in green. Continue until you have found all the ways the lines you drew relate to one another.

(Check students' drawings: intersections [circled] are the points where lines meet; perpendicular lines [red] intersect at right angles; parallel lines [green] do not intersect—the lines are always the same distance apart.)

12. MISSING ANGLES

STANDARDS 1, 3, 9, 10

Look at the pie and the pie pieces labeled *A*, *B*, and *C* in Figure 2 on the Silhouette page (page 74). Think of a way, other than cutting out the pie pieces and fitting them into the empty space, to tell which piece is the one missing from the pie. Try your idea. Which piece is it?

(Answers may vary. Possible answers include: measure the angle of the empty space of the pie and find the piece that has that angle; trace the outline of the empty space of the pie and match its outline to 1 of the pieces; piece A is the missing piece.)

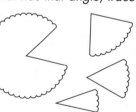

13. PROPERTIES OF POLYGONS

STANDARDS 9, 13

Polygon means *many angles* in Greek. Polygons are closed figures that have 3 or more angles and 3 or more sides. Draw 3 different polygons. Identify the number of sides and angles in each one. What do you notice?

(Polygons drawn will vary; the number of sides in each polygon is equal to the number of angles.)

14. NAMES OF POLYGONS

STANDARDS 4, 9

Write the meaning of each of the following prefixes. You can use a dictionary to help you.

penta hexa hepta octa nona deca

Look at the shapes on the Polygon Card page (Page 75). Write the name of each polygon on it. Choose from the following names: *pentagon, hexagon, heptagon, octagon, nonagon,* and *decagon.*

(penta—5; hexa—6, hepta—7; octa—8; nona—9; deca—10; the pentagon is the 5-sided shape, the hexagon the 6-sided shape, and so on.)

15. POLYGONS RACE

STANDARDS 2, 4, 9

Divide students into teams of 4 or 5. Explain that each team is to name as many examples of polygons as it can in 5 minutes. The team must record the name of the polygon and the example or examples. For instance: octagon—a stop sign.

At the end of 5 minutes, have teams share their lists. If a team lists an example that one or more of the other teams has, the team scores 5 points. If a team lists an example that no other team has, it scores 10 points. The team with the most points wins.

(Examples will vary but may include: triangles— yield signs, rectangles—doors and windows, pentagons—school crossing signs, heptagons— arrows.)

16. SHAPE MEMORY GAME

`STANDARD 9`

Cut out and display the cards from the Polygon Card page (page 75). Allow your partner to look at the cards for an amount of time you both agree to, such as 10 seconds, then cover them. Have your partner try to name the cards that were shown and identify the ones that were missing. Uncover the cards to check the answers. Switch roles and play again.

(Answers will vary.)

17. THE MEANING OF CONCENTRIC SHAPES

`STANDARDS 2, 9`

Concentric shapes have a common center. To draw concentric shapes, outline a large shape on a piece of blank paper. (You can draw a shape with a combination of curved and straight lines, like a square with a half circle above it, or any shape you'd like.) Draw the same outline, only smaller, inside the first outline. Continue drawing smaller and smaller outlines of the shape until you have no more room to draw. How many concentric shapes did you draw?

(Check children's drawings; Number of concentric shapes drawn will vary.)

18. CONCENTRIC SHAPES IN NATURE

STANDARDS 2, 4, 9

Name something in nature that has concentric shapes. Draw it.

(Answers and drawings will vary, but may include: spider's web, ripples made in a puddle when a stone is thrown into it, rings in a log.)

19. TESSELLATIONS

STANDARDS 1, 2, 9

Tessellations are like puzzles. They are patterns made with shapes that fit together without overlapping or leaving spaces. When shapes fit together this way, we say they tessellate.

Cut out the pentagon, hexagon, and octagon shapes from the Polygon Card page (page 75). Using the pentagon, trace it repeatedly, and see if you can draw the outlines so they tessellate, or fit together like pieces of a puzzle. Try it with the heptagon and octagon. Which shapes tessellate?

(The pentagon and hexagon can be made to tessellate.)

20. COMPOSITE SHAPES

STANDARD 3, 9

You can create shapes out of other, smaller shapes. For example, it is possible to arrange 6 triangles to make 1 hexagon.

Use pattern blocks, or draw some shapes of your own. Draw and label the combinations of smaller shapes that make up larger shapes you find. (If you're using pattern blocks, trace them for your drawing.) For example, show a square with a line drawn in it to divide it into 2 triangles. Write *2 triangles make 1 square.*

(Answers will vary.)

A C R O S S   T H E   C U R R I C U L U M

Investigate the Artists (Art)

Abstract artists use lines, shapes, and tessellations in interesting ways. Have individual students or groups research and report on artists such as M.C. Escher, Piet Mondrian, Georges Braque, Henri Matisse, and Alexander Calder.

If possible, plan a field trip to an art museum so students can see examples of the connection between math and art. In addition to abstract drawings and paintings, objects such as tapestries and vases often have patterns showing tessellations and concentric shapes.

21. GEOMETRIC DESIGNS

STANDARDS 2, 9

Draw a picture or design that includes concentric shapes and tessellations. Show your design to your partner. Have your partner find an example of each type of pattern.

(Drawings will vary.)

22. AN INTRODUCTION TO TANGRAMS

STANDARDS 2, 9

Tangrams were invented by the Chinese 4000 years ago. The legend is that a man named Tan was carrying a ceramic tile for the emperor, and he dropped it. He found many wonderful figures and designs to make while he was trying to reassemble the tile. The emperor didn't get his tile, but Tan became the famous inventor of tangrams. All tangrams are made up of 7 pieces that can fit together to form a square.

Look closely at Figure 1, the tangram puzzle, on the Tangram page (page 76), to see how the pieces fit together. Cut out the pieces. Now put the square back together again. Outline each tangram piece in the square you made to show where each piece belongs.

(See tangram puzzle on page 76 for the way the pieces should fit.)

23. DESCRIBING TANGRAM PIECES

STANDARDS 3, 9, 10

Make a list of all the shapes of the tangram pieces (p. 76).
   a. How many different shapes are there?
   b. How many different sizes of triangles?
   c. What pieces, when placed together, form a triangle that matches a large triangle?

(There are 3 different shapes—triangles, a square, and a rhombus; 3 different sizes of triangles; 2 small triangles and the square form a triangle congruent to a large triangle.)

24. MAKING TANGRAM DESIGNS

STANDARD 9

Make a design with your tangram pieces. Show it to your partner and have your partner copy it using his or her own tangram pieces. Take turns making and copying designs.

(Designs will vary.)

25a. A TANGRAM FOX

STANDARDS 3, 9

Look at the fox in Figure 2 on the Tangram page, (page 76). Use your 7 tangram pieces to make

this animal. Outline each tangram piece in your fox shape to show where each piece belongs.

(Note: Children may need to verbalize the steps in the diagram, have them verbalized, or see them modeled.)

25b. A TANGRAM DOG

STANDARDS 3, 9

Change the fox you made into the dog in Figure 3 (page 76) by switching 2 pieces and turning all the other pieces in place. Outline each tangram piece in your dog shape to show where each piece belongs. Color the 2 pieces you switched yellow. Color the pieces you turned in place green.

27. CREATING YOUR OWN PAPER OBJECTS

STANDARDS 2, 3, 9

Create your own paper object by folding a square piece of paper. Then explain how you did it, either by drawing, telling, or writing.

(Objects and explanations will vary.)

26. ORIGAMI

STANDARDS 2, 4, 9

Origami is the art of paper folding, and it comes from Japan. Many beautiful 3-dimensional objects can be made by folding paper. In Japan, people learn origami as children.

To make your own origami cup, cut out the large square from the Origami Cup page (page 77). Copy the letters *A-F* as they appear on the front of the square onto the back of the square too, so that when the paper is folded you can read the letters no matter which side is showing. Follow the steps shown to make a cup. If you'd like to be able to drink out of the cup, make it out of wax paper.

ACROSS THE CURRICULUM

Paper Flowers (Art)

Brighten up the classroom with some colorful tissue or crepe-paper flowers. Follow the directions to make 1 flower:

1. Make a stack of 4-5 square pieces of tissue or crepe paper.
2. Fold the paper accordion style.
3. Twist a pipe cleaner or piece of florist's wire around the middle of the paper, making a "bow tie."
4. Fluff out the layers.

Shapes

Figure 1

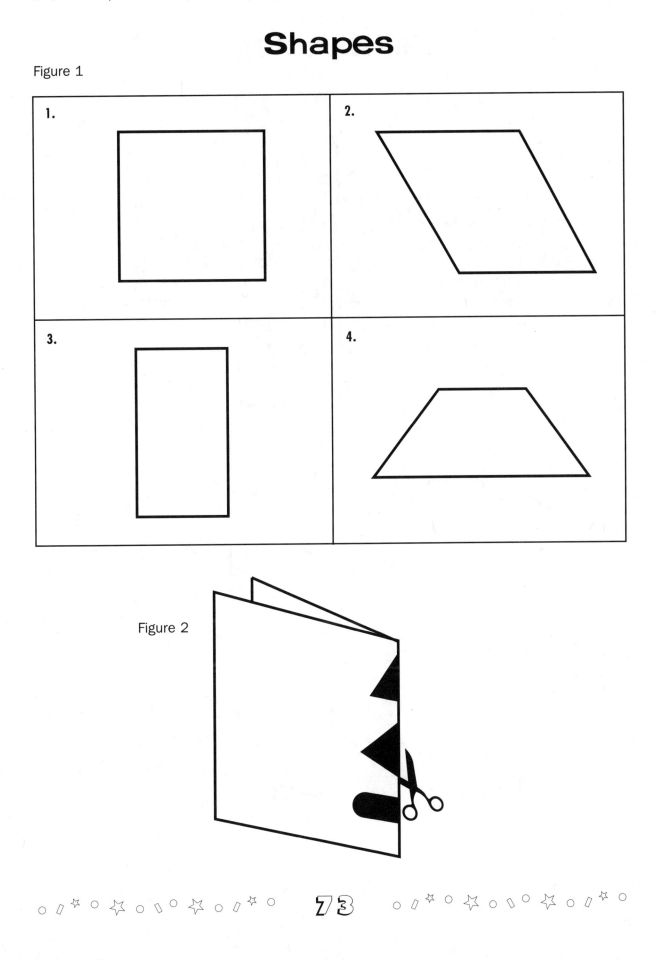

Silhouettes

Figure 1

CUBE

Figure 2

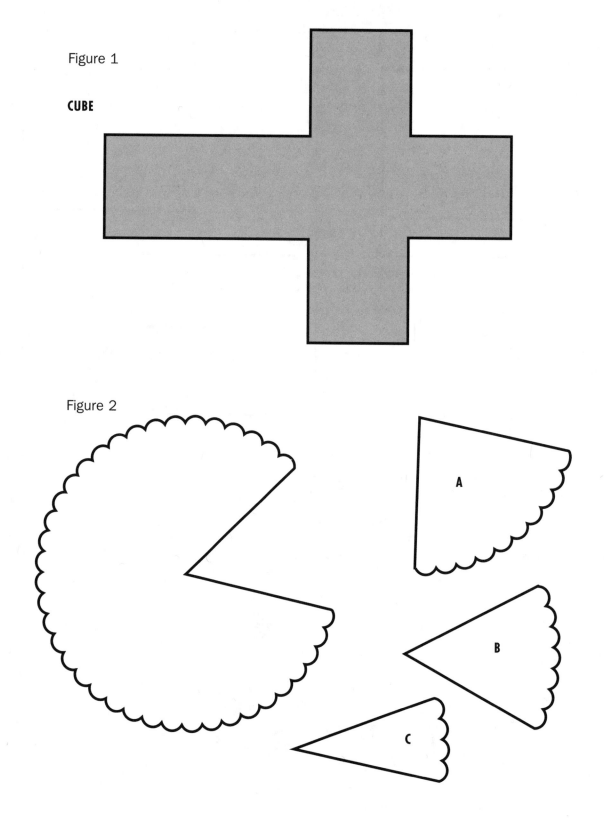

Polygon Card

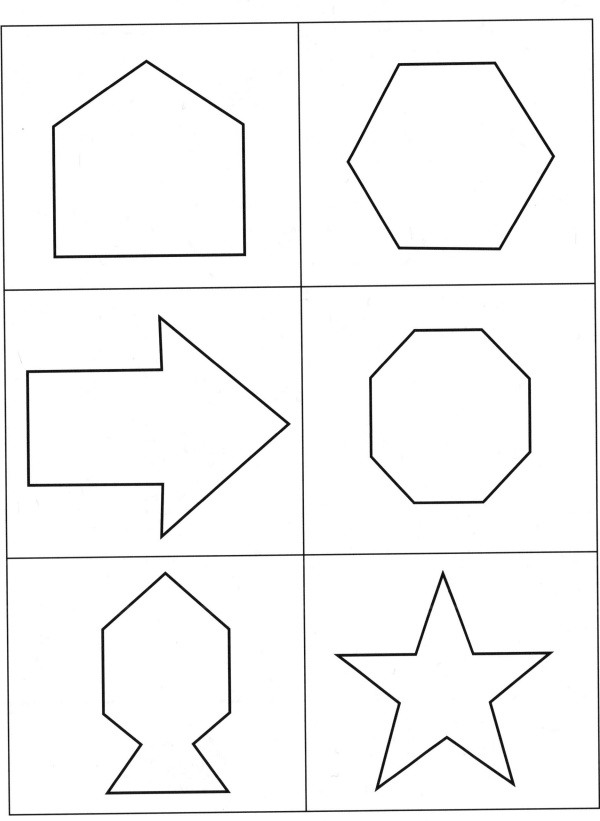

Tangrams

Figure 1

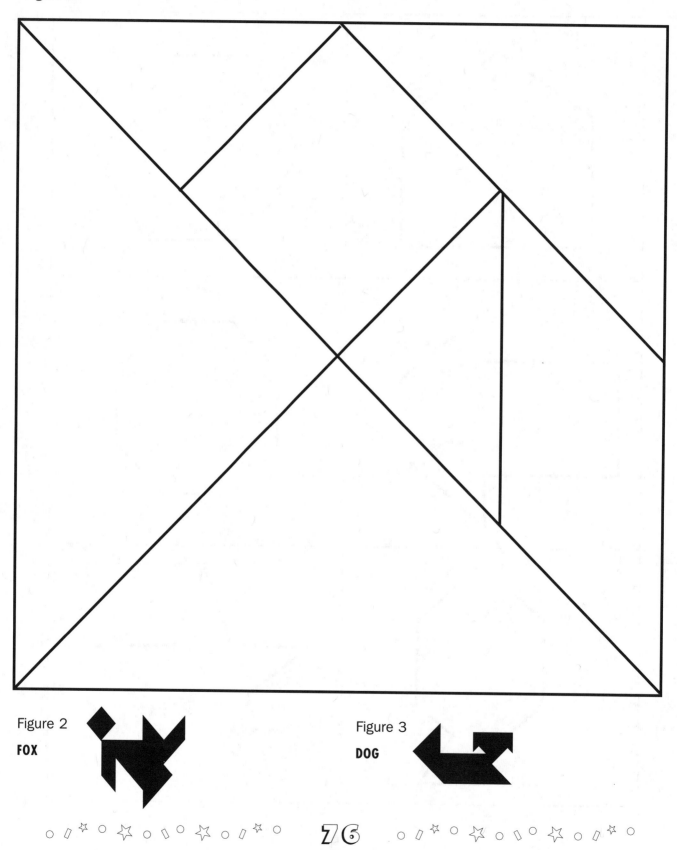

Figure 2

FOX

Figure 3

DOG

Origami Cup

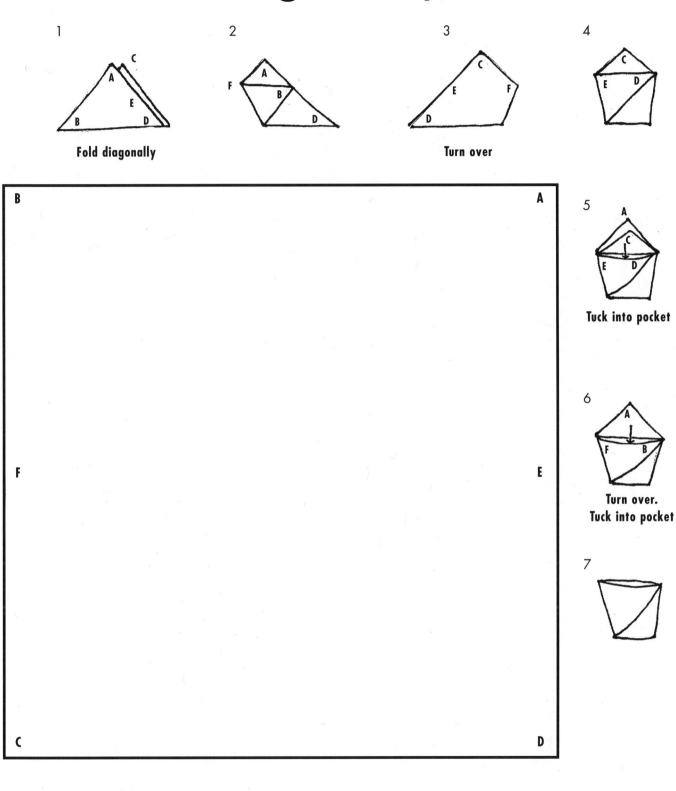

1

A **C**

E

B **D**

Fold diagonally

2

F **A**

B

D

3

C

E

F

D

Turn over

4

C

E **D**

5

A

C

E **D**

Tuck into pocket

6

A

F **B**

Turn over.
Tuck into pocket

7

B **A**

F **E**

C **D**

CHAPTER 8

Charts, Graphs, and Maps

1. BAR GRAPH / HOUSEHOLD CHORES

STANDARDS 2, 11

Make a bar graph to show which household chores students in the class like the most (or mind the least!). Draw a graph similar to the Basic Graph (page 86) on the chalk-board. On the horizontal axis (bottom) write 5 chores, such as *cooking, cleaning, raking leaves, putting things away,* and *washing dishes* (or draw symbols to represent each chore if you like). On the vertical axis (left) write each students' name. Ask each student to choose his or her favorite chore from those listed and to color in 1 box in the appropriate column. Have students copy the information onto individual copies of the graph on page 86.

Have students answer questions on the information shown in the graph, such as, *Which job is liked the most? Which job is liked the least? How many more students like raking leaves than like cleaning?*

(Graphs will vary.)

2. LINE GRAPH / CLASS ATTENDANCE

STANDARDS 4, 11

Make a line graph to show your class' attendance for one week.

Use the Basic Graph (page 86). Along the horizontal axis write the days of the school week. On the vertical axis, starting with 1, write the number of students in your class.

Record daily attendance by finding the line for the day of the week on the bottom of the graph, and the number on the vertical axis that represents the number of students in class that day. Mark the point where these lines intersect with a dot.

At the end of the week, draw a line connecting the dots and describe what this line looks like. What does the line tell you about your class' attendance?

(Check to be sure that students' graphs are accurate.)

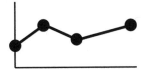

3. CIRCLE GRAPHS / HOBBIES

STANDARDS 8, 11

Look at the circle graph in Figure 1 on the Graph It page (page 87). In a circle graph, each section represents part, or a percentage, of the whole. The entire circle represents one whole, or 100%.

a. Fill in the circle graph to show how much of Daryl's free time he spends on different hobbies. Use the following information:
20% baseball
30% playing drums
30% computer games
10% watching TV
10% drawing

b. Now, make a circle graph that shows how much of your free time you spend on different hobbies.

(Check children's graphs. Individual graphs will vary.)

4. COMPARING TWO HOBBIES

STANDARDS 3, 11

Look at the graph in Figure 2 on the Graph It page (page 87). What is the label on the horizontal, or bottom, axis? What is the label on the vertical, or left, axis? Write 1 or 2 sentences describing what the graph shows about Ralph and Anya.

(Playing Soccer; Drawing; Ralph likes to draw more than he likes playing soccer and more than Anya likes drawing; Anya likes to play soccer more than she likes drawing and more than Ralph likes playing soccer.)

5. MAKING A GRAPH TO COMPARE TWO HOBBIES

STANDARDS 2, 11

Make a graph of your own like the one in Figure 2 on the Graph It page (page 87). Label your graph with two activities and a measuring system such as, *high interest* and *low interest* or *dislike* and *like very much*.

Ask the other members in your group to mark the graph to show how they would rate themselves on the 2 activities. Write 1 or 2 sentences describing what your graph shows.

(Graphs and descriptions will vary.)

6. TAKING A SURVEY

STANDARDS 2, 4, 11

You can conduct surveys to gather information about the likes and dislikes of people in your school. Work with the members in your group to decide what information you would like to gather. Write 3 questions to ask in your survey. You could ask questions about sports, hobbies, foods, music, and so on.

Find 10 people to whom you can ask your survey questions. Graph your survey results.

(Survey questions and answers will vary. Check children's graphs.)

ACROSS THE CURRICULUM

Reading Speed (Reading)

Have children label 3 columns along the horizontal axis of the graph on page 86 *Book 1*, *Book 2*, and *Book 3*. Then have them label the vertical axis from 0 to 200, writing multiples of 10. Time children as they read for 1 minute. Ask them to count the number of words they read (while still understanding the story) and record the result in the first column of their graphs. Have them exchange books and time them and have them count again. Repeat until they have recorded the number of words read in 1 minute for 3 books. Have children suggest a title for their graphs.

Discuss factors that make a difference in reading speed, such as difficulty of material, number and size of pictures, size of print, number of words on a page, and so on.

7. USING COORDINATES TO PLOT POINTS ON A GRID

STANDARDS 9, 11

Look at the grid in Figure 1 on the Grids and Charts page, (page 86). The numbers across the bottom identify positions along the horizontal axis. The letters along the left side identify positions on the vertical axis. A number and a letter together can be used to identify the location of a point on the grid. The number and letter pair are called the **coordinates** of the point.

Draw a dot on the grid to show the point named by each of these coordinates:

9E	8D	8F	7C
7G	6B	6H	5A
5I	4B	4H	3C
3G	2D	2F	1E

Then connect the dots. What shape do you see? Compare your grid with your partner's. If any of your points are in different locations, check the coordinates to see which location is correct.

(The given coordinates form a rhombus, or diamond.)

8. TIC-TAC-DOT

STANDARDS 3, 9

Use the grid in Figure 1 on the Grids and Charts page (page 88) to play a tic-tac-toe game. You and your partner take turns naming coordinates and drawing an X or an O on the grid to mark the point named. The object of the game is to be the first one to get 3 Xs or Os in a row diagonally, vertically, or horizontally.

(Answers will vary.)

9. FOLLOWING AND GIVING DIRECTIONS TO DRAW PICTURES ON THE GRID

STANDARDS 2, 9, 11

Make two grids like the one in Figure 1 on the Grids and Charts page (page 88), but label the *spaces* with numbers and letters instead of the lines. Create a picture or design on one of the grids by coloring in some or all of the boxes.

Without showing your partner what you drew, give him or her the coordinates so that he or she can copy your picture or design onto the blank grid.

(Pictures and designs will vary.)

10. A CATEGORIES GAME

STANDARDS 4, 11

Use the chart in Figure 2, on the Grids and Charts page (page 88) to play a categories game. In the bottom spaces, write the letters *r, m, t,* and *p.* In the spaces along the left, write *food, animal, clothing, sport.* Move up and across to find out what to write in each square. **For example,** in the square where the *t* column intersects with the *food* row, you

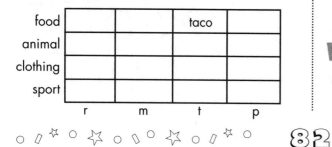

food			taco	
animal				
clothing				
sport				
	r	m	t	p

must write a food that begins with *t,* such as *tacos* or *tomatoes.* Write 2 items in each square.

Compare your chart with the charts of the other members in your group. Score 1 point for each item you have that another group member has too; score 2 points for each item you have that others don't. The person with the greatest number of points wins.

(Charts and scores will vary.)

11. ALWAYS, OFTEN, SOMETIMES, NEVER

STANDARDS 2, 3, 11

Label the spaces along the bottom of the chart in Figure 2 on the Grids and Charts page (page 88) *always, often, sometimes,* and *never.* Write the following activities along the left side of the chart: *do chores, study for tests, eat dessert, go to bed early.* Decide how often you do each of these and put a check in the appropriate box.

Compare your chart with your partner's. Describe how your charts are similar, and how they are different.

(Charts will vary. Similarities and differences will vary.)

12. USING A CHART TO ORGANIZE INFORMATION

STANDARDS 1, 2, 11

Write the steps you would follow to find the answer to the question *In* which month do the greatest number of people in your class have their birthday? How would a chart be helpful?

(Steps will vary, but may include: 1. Write down the birthday of everyone in the class. 2. List the months and make a tally mark next to the month for each birthday. 3. Count the tally marks to find which month has the greatest number. One possible response: A chart would be helpful for listing the months and making a tally.)

ACROSS THE CURRICULUM

o ☆ o ⭐ o ☆ o ☆ o ☆ o ⭐

Hide the Marker (Sports and Recreation)

Have students play this game in groups of 2 to 4. Each player needs a copy of the grid in Figure 1, page 88, and some small marker, such as a centimeter cube. One player hides his or her marker on a point of the grid, keeping the grid out of view of the other players. The other players take turns naming coordinates, trying to guess where the marker is located. If the guess is not correct, the "hider" tells the player one direction to move (up, down, left, right) to go from the coordinates which were guessed to the hidden marker. The players move their own markers according to the clues the hider gives. The player who names the coordinates of the hidden marker hides it for the next game.

INDIVIDUAL
I

13a. MAKING A MAP

STANDARDS 4, 9, 11

Follow these directions to draw a map of a neighborhood:
a. Draw a grid with 3 horizontal lines and 3 vertical lines.

b. Label the horizontal lines from the bottom to the top *1st Street*, *2nd Street*, and *3rd Street*.
c. Label the vertical lines from left to right *Hill Ave.*, *Lake Ave.*, and *Park Ave.*
d. Write an N (for north) at the top of the map, an S (for south) on the bottom, a W (for west) on the left side, and an E (for east) on the right side.
e. Draw a school on the northeast corner of 3rd Street and Hill Ave.
f. Draw a park extending from Lake Ave. to Park Ave., and from 1st Street to 2nd Street.
g. Draw a pond in the southwest corner of the park.

PARTNERS
P

13b. FINDING LOCATIONS ON A MAP

STANDARDS 2, 4, 9, 11

Draw 4 places of interest on the map you made in Exercise 13a, such as a baseball field, an outdoor skating rink, a mall, City Hall, and so on. Take turns with your partner naming the location of each place by identifying streets, avenues, or compass directions. Have your partner point out where it would be located if it were on his or her map.

(Places drawn on maps will vary.)

14. CREATING MAP LEGENDS

STANDARDS 2, 9, 11

Maps often have **legends** which explain what the symbols used on the map represent. Make a grid and draw a map of a city on it. Include 5 different symbols for things in the city such as schools, parks, subway stations, libraries, and so on. Include a legend that tells what each symbol means.

(Maps will vary.)

15. USING SCALE ON A MAP

STANDARDS 1, 5, 9, 10, 11

Maps are smaller than the areas they represent. A scale on a map tells how the measures on the map compare with the actual measures. For example, the scale on a map might be 1 inch equals 16 miles. If the distance between 2 towns on the map is 2 inches, the actual distance is 32 miles. What would be the actual distance if the distance on the map was 1/2 inch?

Work with your partner to draw a large rectangle to use as the outline of a map. Use a scale of 1 centimeter equals 10 kilometers (1cm=10km). You can think of a centimeter as being about equal to the width of your index finger. Label the towns of *Riverville, Lakeville, Blueville,* and *Redville* on your map using the following information:

a. Riverville is 50 km west of Lakeville.
b. Lakeville is 70 km north of Redville.
c. Blueville is about half the distance between Riverville and Redville.

Compare your map with another pair's map. Check that the distances between the towns are about the same. (The location of towns may be different, but distances between them should be about the same.) If they're not about the same, remeasure them.

(8 miles.)

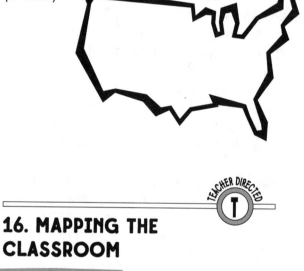

16. MAPPING THE CLASSROOM

STANDARDS 4, 5, 9

Have children work in small groups to draw maps of the classroom. Divide the room into sections, and assign a section to each group (the size of each section will depend on the size of your classroom). Give each group a piece of 12 in. by 18 in. paper. Have students use a scale of 1 inch equals 1 foot. Suggest that students determine about how long a foot (12 inches) is compared to their feet. They can then use that reference measure to estimate the number of feet across the room, between objects, and so on. Put the finished maps together to make a complete map of the room.

(Maps will vary.)

INDIVIDUAL

17. ESTIMATING TO COMPARE DISTANCES BETWEEN TOWNS ON A MAP

STANDARDS 5, 10, 11

Look at the map on page 89. Estimate to compare distances between towns. Copy and complete this sentence at least 3 different ways:

_____ is about as far from _____ as _____ is from _____.

(Answers may vary, but may include: Poptown is about as far from Strawtown as Strawtown is from Globetown; Sandtown is about as far from Poptown as Looptown is from Globetown. Looptown is about as far from Rocktown as Rocktown is from Sandtown.)

18. DESIGNING A DREAM ROOM

STANDARDS 1, 2, 10, 11

Design the room of your dreams. Decide on a scale, such as 1 inch equals 1 foot, or 1 centimeter equals 1 meter. Draw the objects in your room according to that scale. Color and label the furniture in your

dream room. Compare your picture with your partner's. Discuss ways the rooms are alike, and ways they are different.

(Check children's drawings for consistent use of scale.)

ACROSS THE CURRICULUM

Map Collections (Social Studies)

Collect a variety of maps, such as a road map of your city, highway maps of states, a political map of a country, a topographical map of a region, and so on. Display the maps for children to look at during free time. Ask them to compare 2 of the maps and write 3 ways the maps are alike, and 3 ways they are different.

Visit From An Architect (Social Studies)

Ask a parent or another adult who is an architect to visit your class and discuss his or her job, emphasizing how important math is to the profession.

Basic Graph

Graph It

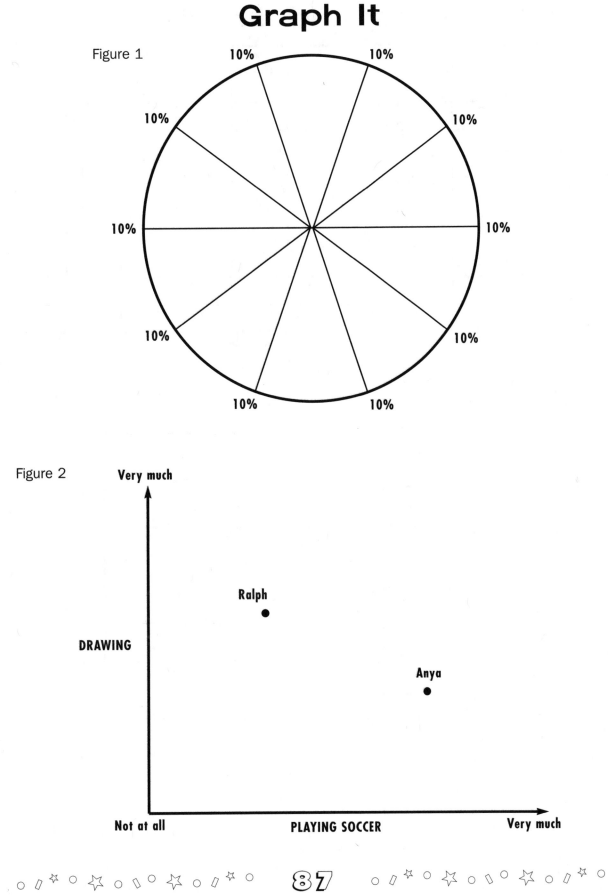

Figure 1

10% 10% 10% 10% 10% 10% 10% 10% 10% 10%

Figure 2

Very much

Ralph

DRAWING

Anya

Not at all   PLAYING SOCCER   Very much

Grids and Charts

Figure 1

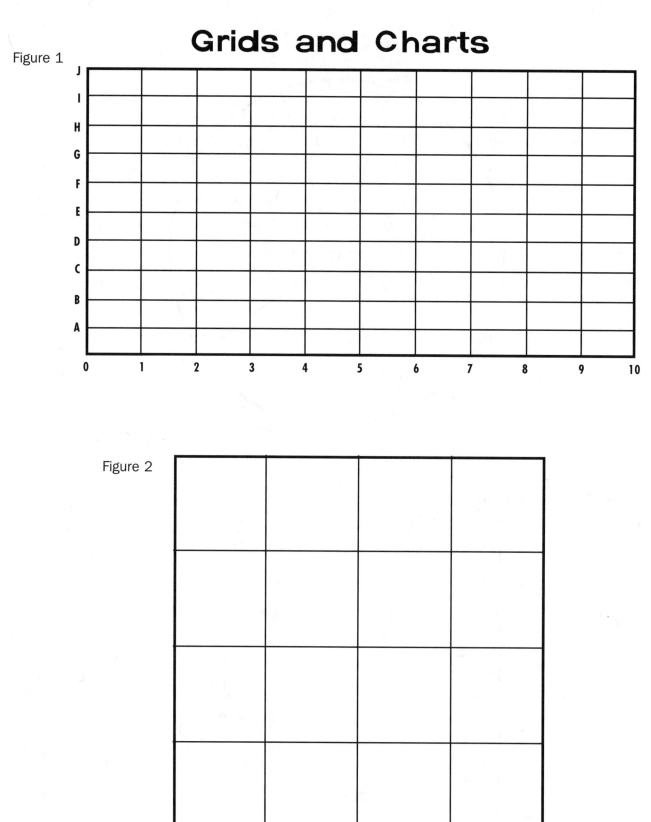

Figure 2

Maps and Diagrams

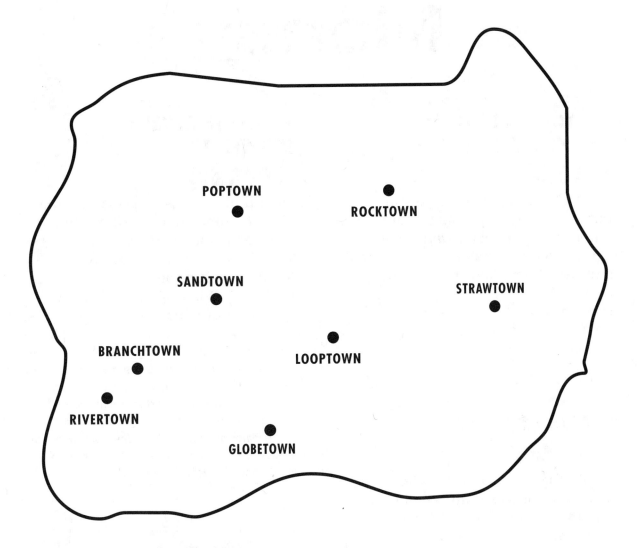

Time and Money

1. CYCLES IN NATURE AND MEASURING TIME

STANDARDS 4, 10

Long ago, people used cycles in nature to tell the passing of time and seasons. Explain what time periods people measured using the sun, the moon, and the seasons.

(Sun—hours and days, moon—days and months, seasons—years.)

2. DAYS IN A YEAR

STANDARDS 4, 8, 10

Would the number of days in a year be greater or less than 365 if each month had 30 days? Why does a year last for 365 days? Do some research to find out why we have leap year every 4 years.

(Less than; that's about how long it takes Earth to complete 1 orbit around the sun; the time it takes Earth to orbit the sun is closer to 365 1/4 days than 365 days, so every 4 years (leap year); a day is added to adjust the calendar.)

3. TIME MEASURED IN TWELFTHS

STANDARDS 4, 10

The number 12 is a special number when it comes to measuring time. Work with your partner to name at least 2 ways we measure time in twelfths, or numbers that are divisible by 12. What other numbers do we use to measure time?

(Answers may vary, but may include: There are 12 months in a year; days are measured by a multiple of 12 [24 hours in a day]; seconds and minutes are measured in a multiple of 12 [60 seconds in a minute, 60 minutes in an hour]; other numbers used to measure time may include: 7—days in a week; 4—weeks in a month and quarters in an hour.)

4. DESIGNING A TIME MEASUREMENT SYSTEM

STANDARDS 2, 3, 4, 10

Suppose you can change the way time is measured. Work with your group to write a short story telling what changes you would make, and how the instruments we use to measure time, such as clocks and calendars, would be different.

(Answers will vary.)

5. DAYS IN A MONTH

STANDARDS 8, 10

Answer the following questions without looking at a calendar:

a. If the first day of the month is a Monday, what will be the dates of the other Mondays in the month?

b. If the first day of the month is Sunday, what will be the date of the first Saturday?

Write a calendar problem of your own. Trade problems with your partner and solve. Check each other's answers.

(Other Mondays: 8th, 15th, 22nd, 29th; if Sunday is the 1st, the first Saturday will be the 7th; problems will vary.)

6. COMPARING MARS YEARS AND EARTH YEARS

STANDARDS 4, 8, 10

It takes Mars 687 Earth days to orbit once around the sun. So, 1 year on Mars is 687 Earth days. About how many Earth years is 687 days?

Use a calculator to determine about how many days old you are. How many years old would you be if Earth years were as long as Mars years?

(A year on Mars is nearly twice as long as a year on Earth; number of days old and age in Mars years will vary depending on age, but age in Mars years will be roughly half of age in Earth years. For example, a child who is 10 years old is about 3,650 days old. That's a little more than 5 years in Mars years.)

ACROSS THE CURRICULUM

Make a Sundial (Science)

Follow these directions to make a sundial. You may wish to have each small group make a sundial, or make 1 sundial together as a class.

a. Place a dowel in the ground where there is sunlight all day long.

b. Draw a circle around it.

c. Mark and label the places on the circle the shadow points toward at 9:00 A.M., 10:00 A.M., 11:00 A.M., 12:00 noon, 1:00 P.M., 2:00 P.M., and so on.

Check the sundial against a clock or watch daily, making adjustments until it is accurate.

Ask questions about the experience, such as, *When does the shadow increase in length? Decrease in length? Is there a time when the shadow nearly disappears?* (The further from noon the hour is, either earlier or later, the longer the shadow. The shadow nearly disappears at noontime.)

7. INVENTIONS OF THE PAST 200 YEARS

PARTNERS P

STANDARDS 4, 10

Tortoises live longer than any other animal. Some tortoises live to be 200 years old! Suppose you were born 200 years ago. Work with your partner to list 5 things that would have been invented or discovered during your lifetime. You can use an almanac or encyclopedia to help.

(Answers will vary, but may include: telephone, television, microcomputer, radio, microwave, automobile, train, airplane.)

8. WORK SHIFTS

SMALL GROUP S

STANDARDS 2, 4, 10

Make a chart showing whether people in the following jobs work during the daytime hours, the nighttime hours, or both: a cook, a teacher, a police officer, a secretary, a security guard, a bank teller, a grocery clerk, a doctor, a firefighter, a mail carrier.

Compare your group's chart with another group's.

(Answers may vary. One possible answer: daytime hours—a teacher, a secretary, a bank teller, a mail carrier; nighttime hours exclusively—none; both daytime and nighttime hours—a cook, a grocery clerk, a doctor, a firefighter.)

9. BIRTH DATES

INDIVIDUAL I

STANDARDS 4, 10

Peg and Greg are twins. Peg was born at 11:57 P.M. on December 31, 1990. Greg was born 7 minutes later. Draw a clock to show when each one was born. What is Peg's birth date? Greg's birth date?

(The clock for Peg should show 11:57, the clock for Greg 12:04; Peg's birth date is 12/31/90, Greg's birth date is 1/1/91.)

10. MAKING A GAME SCHEDULE

INDIVIDUAL I

STANDARDS 4, 8, 10

The Little Sluggers baseball games last 1 hour and 30 minutes. The coaches need to schedule 5 games on 1 baseball field on a Saturday. All teams must be off the field by 5:00. Make a schedule to show when each of the 5 games can be played.

(Answers will vary according to starting time and whether any time is allowed between games. One possible schedule, allowing 15 minutes between games: Game 1—8:30, Game 2—10:15, Game 3—12:00, Game 4—1:45, Game 5—3:30.)

11. MAKING A PARTY SCHEDULE

PARTNERS P

STANDARDS 4, 8, 10

LaJean is having a party. She wants her guests to spend some time swimming, eating lunch, and watching a movie. Everyone will be doing the same activity at the same time. The party starts at 11:00 and ends at 2:00.

Which activity should take the longest amount of time? The shortest? Write a schedule for LaJean's party. Compare your schedule with your partner's. Should they be the same? Explain.

(Answers will vary; schedules will vary. One possible schedule: 11:00-12:30—movie, 12:30-1:30—swim, 1:30-2:00—eat lunch; schedules don't have to be the same.)

12. MAKING AN AFTER-SCHOOL SCHEDULE

STANDARDS 4, 8, 10

On Fridays, Sonja's class always has a test. The teacher asks the children to study about 2 hours during the week for the test. Sonja likes to play outside in the afternoons, and her bedtime is 8:30. Sonja reads for 30 minutes every night.

Together with your partner, write an after-school schedule for Sonja that includes her study time, the other activities mentioned, and other things Sonja might do in the evenings.

(Schedules will vary. One possible schedule:

TIME	ACTIVITY
after school until 6:00	play outside
6:00-6:30	eat dinner
6:30-7:00	study
7:00-8:00	do chores, talk on phone, get ready for bed, and so on
8:00-8:30	read

13. 24-HOUR CLOCK

STANDARDS 3, 8, 10

In the military, people use a 24-hour clock. Look at the chart in Figure 1 on the Military Time page (page 98). Midnight is 00 hours, 1 A.M. is 0100 hours, 2 A.M. is 0200 hours, and so on.

Write numbers on a clock face the way you are used to seeing them. Now draw another clock face and on it write military times. When the hands on a military clock have gone around once, how many times have the hands on a 12-hour clock gone around?

(Check students' clocks—the numbers 1 to 12 should be written on one clock face, the numbers 00 to 2300 should be written on the other. The hands on a 12-hour clock go around twice for every 1 time around on a military clock.)

14. WRITING A SCHEDULE USING MILITARY TIME

STANDARDS 4, 10

Use the chart in Figure 1 on the Military Time page (page 98) to rewrite your class schedule using military time.

(Schedules will vary.)

15. ESTIMATING TIME

STANDARDS 5, 8, 10

Lupe groaned as he looked at the clock after he and his mother and two sisters finished a spaghetti dinner. His favorite TV show was starting, and it was his night to do the dishes! Lupe estimates it takes him 10 seconds to wash each glass, 30 seconds to wash each dirty dish, and 1 minute to wash each dirty pan or serving bowl. He can wash all the silverware in 5 minutes. He needs to wash:

1 spaghetti pot
1 tomato sauce pot
1 salad bowl
silverware, a glass, a salad plate, a dinner plate, and a dessert bowl per person

About how many minutes of Lupe's favorite program will he miss?

(Estimates may vary. He will miss about 15 minutes of his favorite program. He spends about 10 seconds + 90 seconds, or 100 seconds, on each person's glass and dishes. For 4 people that's 400 seconds, or about 7 minutes. He spends about 3 minutes doing the pots and serving bowl, and 5 minutes doing the silverware. 7 min + 3 min + 5 min = 15 min.)

16. OBJECTS USED AS MONEY

STANDARDS 4, 8, 10

Money has been in use for a very, very long time. People used shells, stones, clay, and other objects for money before it was made from metal and paper.

Suppose peanuts were used for money. If 3 peanuts are equal in value to a penny, how many peanuts equal a nickel? A dime? A quarter? Would the value of 100 peanuts be greater than or less than 40¢?

(15 peanuts = 1 nickel; 30 peanuts = 1 dime; 75 peanuts = 1 quarter; the value of 100 peanuts would be less than 40¢.)

A C R O S S   T H E   C U R R I C U L U M

World Records (Social Studies)

Provide children with the following information: A group of college students claim to have made the longest phone call in the world—they talked for over 720 hours.

Have children determine how many days that is (30 days). Have children work in small groups using a world's record book, or books, to research 3 other unusual things people have done for a record amount of time. Make a class chart showing the record time for each event.

17. CREATING A MONEY SYSTEM

STANDARDS 1, 3, 6, 10

Work with your partner to invent a money system, using objects from nature in place of coins or dollar bills. For example, 5 pebbles might equal 1 shell. It might cost 2 shells to buy a soda. Write or draw a description of your money system showing how many of 1 object it takes to equal the value of another object. Also, show the price of three things, such as an ice cream cone, a movie, and a pair of jeans using your system.

*(Answers will vary.
Students may set up a system in which value is related to size—the smaller the object, the lesser the value, and it may take several small objects to equal the value of a large object.)*

18. IDENTIFYING COINS

STANDARDS 4, 10

Use the first row of coin cards on page 99. Look at the president pictured on each coin. Arrange the coins in the order described by these clues:

a. The 2 most famous presidents are facing each other.
b. The president with a beard is first.
c. The 2 presidents with pony tails are next to each other.
d. The most recent president is last.

Write the coins in order. What is the value of the 4 coins together?

(The order is: penny [Lincoln], quarter [Washington], nickel [Jefferson], dime [Roosevelt]; the value of the 4 coins is 41 cents.)

19. MATCHING COINS AND AMOUNTS

STANDARDS 10, 12

Use the coin cards (page 99) to find the card or combination of cards for each problem. Record the name and number of coins shown on each card.

a. Find 3 coins that can be combined to equal 40¢.
b. Find 11 coins that can be combined to equal 15¢.
c. Find 4 coins that can be combined to equal 12¢.
d. Find 4 coins that can be combined to equal 50¢.
e. Find 5 coins that can be combined to equal 18¢.

(a. quarter/dime card and nickel card; b. 10 pennies card and nickel card; c. 2 nickels card and 2 pennies card; d. quarter/dime card and dime/nickel card; e. dime/nickel card and 3 pennies card.)

20. DIFFERENT WAYS TO SHOW 25¢

STANDARDS 1, 10, 12

Look at the coin cards (page 99) and record 10 different ways you can show 25¢ using the cards.

(Answers will vary.)

21. COIN GAME

STANDARDS 10, 12

You will each need your own set of coin cards (page 99) to play the coin game. Each player shuffles his or her set of cards and places the cards in a stack, facedown. Next, each player turns over the top card on his or her stack at the same time. The player whose card shows the greatest amount of money records that amount. The first player to reach $2.00 or more, wins.

(Answers will vary.)

ACROSS THE CURRICULUM

○ ☆ ○ ▢ ○ ☆ ○ ▢ ○ ▢ ○ ☆ ○ ▢ ▢ ○ ☆ ○

Money Around the World (Social Studies)

Have children find out what money is called in other countries, and compare its value to the U.S. dollar. (The foreign money exchange rates can be found on the financial pages of most newspapers.) If possible, bring in, or have children bring in, currency from other countries. Display the money and discuss similarities and differences.

22. DECISION MAKING

STANDARDS 1, 3, 4

Raul and Ariel are going to spend 2 hours at an amusement park. The park has food booths, game booths, and rides. They each have $10 to spend. They each have a choice of pay-ing 75¢ for each ride, or paying $10.00 for an unlimited number of rides. What do Raul and Ariel need to think about in order to make their decision?

(Answers will vary. One possible response: Raul and Ariel need to think about whether they want to spend any money on food or games, and whether they have enough time to make the unlimited number of rides worth-while. In considering time they should think about the number of rides they want to go on, how long they would have to wait in line for each ride, and how long each ride may take.)

23. DETERMINING SAVINGS USING A CALENDAR

STANDARDS 1, 4, 12

Charlene wants to save her money for a CD that costs $15.00. Charlene has a $3.00 allowance which she gets on Monday each week. She also has a job walking the neighbor's dog once a day. Each time she walks the dog, she receives $1.00. If she saves all of her money each week, how long will it take her to save enough money to buy the CD? How long would it take her to save enough money to buy 2 CD's at the same price?

(9 days—over a Monday to Sunday period, Charlene can earn $10.00: $3 allowance + $1 per day for 7 days of dog walking. In the next 2 days, Monday and Tuesday, she will earn the additional $5 she needs—$3 allowance + $1 per day for 2 days of dog walking; 21 days—earning $10 a week, it will take her 3 weeks to save $30 to buy 2 CD's.)

24. MAKING A PURCHASE

`STANDARDS 10, 12`

Look at what is for sale in the shop windows of the Mini Mall (page 100). Suppose you won a $50.00 gift certificate.

a. What are 2 different ways you could spend all or some of the $50 at the Mini Mall? Write what you would buy and the cost.

b. How much more money would you need to buy a pair of in-line skates? A dollhouse kit?

(Answers will vary, but total cost in either answer shouldn't exceed $50; $9.95 more for skates; $79.98 more for dollhouse kit.)

	Sale Price	Regular Price
2 CD's	$21.00	$25.98
Running Shoes	$25.75	$51.50
In-Line Skates	$59.95	$119.90
Helmet	$19.99	$39.98
Doll house and 4 Dolls	$129.98	$129.98
3 Books	$12.00	$14.55

(Delia's Dollhouses shouldn't be advertising sale prices.)

25. COMPARING REGULAR PRICES AND SALE PRICES

`STANDARDS 3, 12`

The Mini Mall shops (page 100) are advertising sales. Make a table with a partner to compare the regular prices with the sale prices. Use the following information:

a. Each CD is regularly priced at $12.99.

b. Everything in the sporting goods store is half the regular price.

c. Dollhouses usually sell for $89.98, and dolls are $10.00 each.

d. Paperback books are normally $4.85.

Which store shouldn't be advertising its prices as sale prices?

26. MAKING CHANGE

`STANDARDS 2, 10, 12`

Suppose you are a cashier. Tell what change you would give. Use mental math when you can.

Someone gives you:
a. $1 for a 15¢ item.
b. $5 for something that costs $3.99.
c. $10 for 2 items that cost $5.60 and $4.40.
d. $20 for 3 items that cost $6.25 each.

Which ones did you solve using mental math?

Write 4 problems of your own. Have your partner solve them.

(a. 85¢; b. $1.01; c. no change; d. $1.25; answers may vary from all the problems to none of the problems; written problems will vary.)

Military Time

12 midnight	= 00 hours	12 noon	= 1200 hours
12:30 A.M.	= 0030 hours	12:30 P.M.	= 1230 hours
1 A.M.	= 0100 hours	1 P.M.	= 1300 hours
2 A.M.	= 0200 hours	2 P.M.	= 1400 hours
3 A.M.	= 0300 hours	3 P.M.	= 1500 hours
4 A.M.	= 0400 hours	4 P.M.	= 1600 hours
5 A.M.	= 0500 hours	5 P.M.	= 1700 hours
6 A.M.	= 0600 hours	6 P.M.	= 1800 hours
7 A.M.	= 0700 hours	7 P.M.	= 1900 hours
8 A.M.	= 0800 hours	8 P.M.	= 2000 hours
9 A.M.	= 0900 hours	9 P.M.	= 2100 hours
10 A.M.	= 1000 hours	10 P.M.	= 2200 hours
11 A.M.	= 1100 hours	11 P.M.	= 2300 hours

Coin Cards

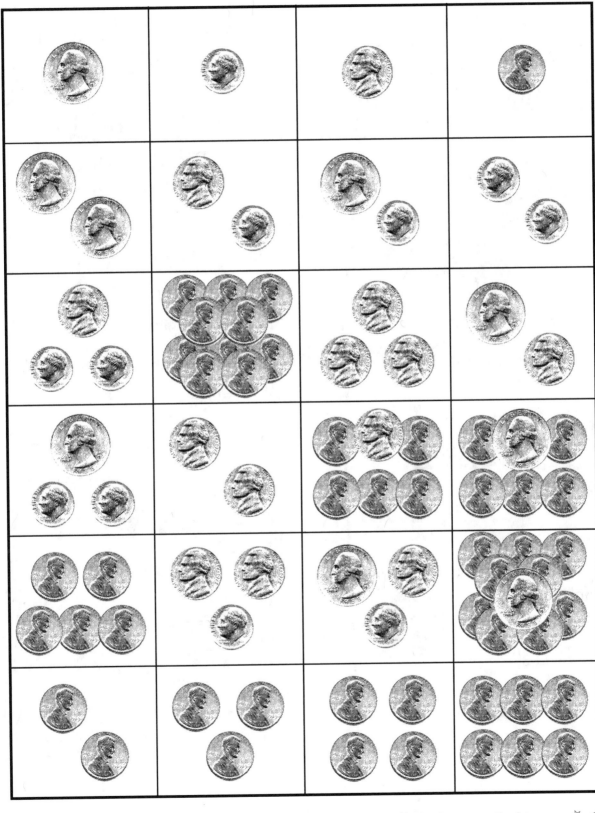

Mini Mall

MIGUEL'S MUSIC

SALE!
2 CDs for only
$21.00!

SPUD'S SPORTS

SALE!

EVERYTHING IN THE STORE IS HALF OFF!

Running Shoes: Now $25.75

In-Line Skates: Just $59.95

Helmets: Only $19.99

DELIA'S DOLLHOUSES

HURRY! SALE!

Just in ... complete
dollhouse kit!
Includes 4 dolls!
Won't Last!!

$129.98

Best Ever Books

SPECIAL Today Only!

3 paperbacks for
$12.00!

Measurement

1. NON-STANDARD UNITS OF MEASURE

STANDARDS 1, 2, 10

Long ago, people measured length using the length of their own feet as the unit of measure. Since people have different sizes of feet, this caused some problems. Write a short story about a problem that occurred because people used their feet to measure. Tell how they solved the problem.

(Stories will vary. Solutions will likely involve the creation or use of a standard unit of measure.)

2. USING NON-STANDARD UNITS OF MEASURE

STANDARDS 1, 2, 10

Ask children to suppose they are living a long time ago—before rulers or yardsticks were used. Ask groups to decide what they would use to measure:

a. the length of a fish.
b. the length of a cow from nose to tail.
c. the height of a tree.

Have groups act out their solutions.

(Answers will vary but children should suggest using different units of measure for each: a larg-

er unit of measure for the cow than the fish, and for the tree than the cow.)

3. UNUSUAL UNITS OF MEASURE

STANDARDS 2, 4, 10

Some unusual units are used for measuring very specific things. For example, the height of horses is measured in *hands.* One *hand* equals 4 inches. The speed of a boat is measured in *knots.* One *knot* equals 6,076 feet.

Working with your partner, make up a unit of measurement. Name the unit of measurement and tell what it would be equal to in length, volume, speed, or distance. Tell what it would be used to measure, and give some sample measurements.

(Answers will vary.)

4. WEIGHT VERSUS VOLUME

STANDARD 10

Find out how cereal in a cereal box is measured. Why does a box of cereal sometimes not feel very full compared to another box the same size?

(Cereal is measured by weight [ounces]. Two boxes the same size may not hold the same amount, but will weigh the same.)

5. ACCURATE MEASURES

STANDARDS 4, 10

Work with 2 or more students to brainstorm situations for which it is very important to have accurate measurements. Make a list of 4 situations.

(Some possible answers: building houses, making clothing, giving medicine, planning a space shuttle flight.)

6. MEASURING SOUND

STANDARDS 4, 10

Sounds we hear are measured in **decibels.** The softest sound humans can hear is about 0 decibels. A normal speaking tone is about 60 decibels. Humans find it very uncomfortable to listen to a sound measuring 130 decibels.

Think of 4 different sounds. Write them in order from softest to loudest. Copy the decibel scale shown. Write your 4 sounds on the scale where you think they belong.

(Answers will vary.)

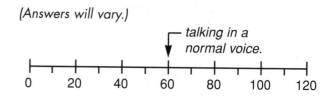

7. ESTIMATION • COMPARING MEASURES

STANDARDS 5, 10

Use the Comparison Cards (page 109) to make estimates about objects in your classroom. Then compare the objects to see if your estimates were correct.

(Answers will vary.)

A C R O S S   T H E   C U R R I C U L U M

Measure Treasure Hunt (Physical Education)

Divide the class into small groups. Ask each group to find two things that:
  a. weigh less than a textbook.
  b. are thicker than a piece of chalk.
  c. can hold more liquid than a coffee mug.

Supermarket Survey (Nutrition/Science)

Have children bring in lists of 5 or 6 food items and the units used to measure them. For example, soda may be measured in ounces or liters; milk is measured in pints, quarts, and gallons; sugar is often measured in pounds.

8. ESTIMATING LENGTH

STANDARDS 5, 10

Estimate how many pennies placed in a row it would take to measure 1 foot. Check your estimate.

(Estimates will vary. It takes 16 pennies to measure 1 foot.)

9. COMPARING CIRCUMFERENCES

STANDARD 10

Describe a way to measure the distance around your wrist.

Find an object the distance around which is longer than the distance around your wrist, but shorter than the distance around your head. What shape is the object?

(With a length of string or a tape measure; objects will vary; shape may be described as round, like a cylinder, or like a sphere.)

10. REFERENCE MEASURES

STANDARD 10

You may not know it, but your hand is a convenient ruler! For most people, the width of the index fingertip is about 1 centimeter. And most people

have 1 finger on which the distance from the top knuckle to the fingertip is 1 inch. Use a ruler to find out for which of your fingers this is true.

Use your "built-in ruler" to find the length of your pencil and 2 other things at your desk. Record the answers both in inches and centimeters. Then check your answers using a real ruler.

(Answers will vary.)

11. INCH, FOOT, YARD

STANDARDS 8, 10

If 12 inches equal 1 foot, and 3 feet equal 1 yard, then how many inches equal 1 yard?

Find 3 things in the classroom that each measure about 1 yard. Find 2 things in the classroom that *together* measure about 1 yard. Record what you find.

Compare your list with your partner's. Check each other's measures.

(There are 36 inches in a yard; lists will vary.)

12. USING INCHES, FEET, AND YARDS

STANDARDS 4, 10

Write 2 things that you would measure using inches, 2 things you would measure using feet, and 2 things you would measure using yards.

(Answers may vary, but may include: inches—pencils, jeans [waist and inseam measurements]; feet—people's heights, rooms in homes; yards—football fields, distances on playground.)

PARTNERS
P

13. MAKING AND ADJUSTING ESTIMATES OF LENGTH

STANDARDS 5, 10

Suppose 10 students stood next to each other and held hands, stretching their arms as far as possible. Estimate how long the line they make would measure.

Work with a partner. Stretch out your arms and measure the distance from fingertip to fingertip. How can you use this information to estimate the length of 10 students' outstretched arms? What is your new estimate?

Which do you think is the better estimate, your first estimate or your second estimate? Explain.

(Estimates will vary; you can multiply the measure of your own outstretched arms by 10; estimates will vary; explanations will vary, but students should recognize that an estimate based on a known measure will more likely be closer to the actual measure than an estimate not based on a known measure.)

ACROSS THE CURRICULUM

○ ☆ ○ ◻ ☆ ○ ☆ ○ ◻ ○ ☆ ○ ◻ ☆ ○ ☆ ○ ◻ ○ ☆ ○ ◻ ☆ ○ ☆ ○ ◻ ○ ☆ ○

Go the Distance (Sports and Recreation)
Make a 10-foot measuring rope by tying a knot at 1 end of a clothesline. Tie additional knots at 1-foot intervals, so that there are 11 knots in all. Cut off any extra clothesline at each end. Children can count the knots to measure how far they can broad jump or travel in 3 hops.

Metric Debate (Social Studies)
Nearly every country in the world except the United States uses the metric system of measurement exclusively. American scientists use the metric system, and so do Olympic athletes.

Discuss the advantages of countries using the same measurement system. Elicit that metric measure equivalencies are based on multiples of ten—10 millimeters equal 1 centimeter, 100 centimeters equal 1 meter, and so on. Have children compare that to customary measure equivalencies. Ask them which system of equivalencies they think is easier to remember.

Brainstorm a list of things that would need to change if the United States were to use the metric system exclusively. Some examples are: mileage signs on roadways, weight information on food packages, reporting of rainfall and snowfall, and so on.

14. IF YOU WERE 30 INCHES TALL

STANDARDS 3, 4, 10

The smallest dinosaur that ever lived was probably the **Compsagnathus.** It was only about 30 inches tall. Find something that is about that height. Record what you find.

Suppose you were 30 inches tall.
a. List 3 things in the room that would be taller than you.
b. Name 2 things you often do at school that would be difficult or impossible to do.
c. Name 2 things that you could do that would be difficult or impossible to do if you were your normal height.

(List of things taller than 30 inches will vary; answers of things impossible to do will vary, as will list of things that would be possible to do.)

15. PERIMETER

STANDARDS 9, 10

Work with your partner to cut out the squares in Figure 1, (page 110). Each square is 1 inch long and 1 inch wide. Make a figure with 8 squares. (Make sure that any 2 squares that are placed next to each other touch along the entire side.)

Measure the distance around the figure you made by counting the outside edges of the squares. (Remember, the length of the side of each square is 1 inch.) The distance around a figure is called the **perimeter.**

Make a different figure using the 8 squares. Does the perimeter change? Use the 8 squares to make a figure with the greatest perimeter you can. What is the perimeter? Make a figure with the least perimeter you can. What is the perimeter?

(Perimeters will vary; the perimeter may or may not change; the greatest perimeter of a figure they can make is 18 inches—a 1 x 8 rectangle; the least perimeter of a figure they can make is 12 inches—a 2 x 4 rectangle.)

16. ESTIMATING PERIMETER

STANDARDS 5, 10

Estimate the perimeter of a book. Now use a ruler to measure the exact perimeter. How does the actual measure compare with your estimate?

Estimate the perimeter of your desk, then measure its perimeter. Estimate, then measure the perimeter of your teacher's desk.

As objects get larger, does it get easier or harder to make an estimate? Explain.

(Comparisons will vary; explanations will vary.)

17. ESTIMATING LENGTH

STANDARDS 5, 8, 10

Estimate how many centimeters long your foot is. Estimate whether the length of each of your fingers and thumb on 1 hand, added together, is more or less than the length of your foot. Measure to the nearest centimeter to check your estimates.

(Estimates will vary. It is most likely that the sum of finger and thumb lengths will be greater than the length of the foot.)

18. IDENTIFYING AN OBJECT BY LENGTH

STANDARDS 3, 10

Look at the pictures on the Object Page (page 111). Read the following clues to find the mystery object:

The mystery object is longer than 10 cm. It is not the longest object but it has the greatest perimeter. What is it?

(The mystery object is the calculator. The length is 12 cm, the perimeter is 42 cm.)

19. DESCRIBING OBJECTS USING MEASUREMENTS

STANDARDS 2, 3, 10

Using the objects on the Object Page (page 111), make up your own measurement mystery. Give your partner the clues and have him or her guess your mystery object.

(Clues and mystery objects will vary.)

20. AREA

STANDARDS 9, 10

When you find how much space a figure covers you are finding the **area** of the figure. It is measured in square units. Use all 25 of the 1-inch squares in Figure 1 (page 110) to make 3 separate figures. What is the area of each figure?

Use all 25 inch squares to make each of 3 different figures. Trace around the outside of your figures, record each area, and color them.

(Figures will vary but the area of each figure will be 25 square inches.)

21. AREA AND PERIMETER

STANDARDS 9, 10,13

Work with a partner to make different figures using the square inches in Figure 1 (page 110). Record the perimeter and area of the figures you make in the chart in Figure 2 (page 110).

Write a letter to a friend telling what you know about perimeter and area.

(Charts will vary; letters will vary, but may include: the area is the same as the number of inch squares used to make a figure; figures with the same area can have different perimeters; to find the area of a rectangle, you can multiply length times width; to find perimeter, you add the lengths of all the sides of a figure.)

22. COMPARING AREAS AND PERIMETERS

STANDARDS 5, 9, 10

Look at the shapes on page 112. Predict which ones have the same area and which ones have the same perimeter. Use the grid on top of the page to check your predictions. (Each square of the grid is 1 square centimeter.) Make a table like the one in Figure 2 (page 110) to record the measures.

(Predictions will vary. Shapes A, B, D, E, and F all have areas of 12 sq. cm; shapes A, C, and D all have perimeters of 16 cm.)

Figure	Area (sq. cm)	Perimeter (cm)
A	12	16
B	12	14
C	16	16
D	12	16
E	12	26
F	12	18

23. METER TAPE MEASURES

STANDARDS 5, 10

Put two 100 cm lengths of masking tape together, sticky sides facing each other, for each student pair. Have each pair use a ruler to mark each centimeter from 1 to 100 (starting from the left end), labeling multiples of 5 (5, 10, 15, 20, and so on). Students can color alternating sections of 10 centimeters (from 0 to 10 cm, from 11 to 20 cm, from 21 to 30 cm, and so on) different colors to make it easier to read the tape measure.

Have children use the tape measures to find items in the room that are about 1 meter in length. Then point out objects in the classroom and ask students to estimate whether they are greater than or less than 1 meter in length. Have volunteers use their tape measures to check the answers.

(Objects chosen and estimates will vary.)

24. COMPARING SIZE

STANDARDS 3, 10

Close your eyes and picture a jar filled with small marbles. Now picture a jar the same size filled with large marbles. Open your eyes and draw a picture of what you saw. Which jar do you think holds more marbles? Explain why you think this.

(Check students' drawings. Students should recognize that the same-size jar will hold a greater number of small objects than large objects.)

25. EQUIVALENT MEASURES

STANDARDS 4, 8, 10, 12

Copy the table below. Use the following information to complete it.

16 tablespoons = 1 cup   1 gallon = 4 quarts
1 quart = 4 cups   1 pint = 2 cups

TABLE OF MEASURES

Unit of Measure	Number of Ounces
1 tablespoon	
1 cup	8
1 pint	
1 quart	
1 gallon	

(1 tablespoon = 1/2 ounce, 1 cup = 8 ounces, 1 pint = 16 ounces, 1 quart = 32 ounces, 1 gallon = 128 ounces.)

26. MEASURING WEIGHT

STANDARDS 1, 3, 10

At a grocery store, a sign says that apples are 99¢ a pound. If you didn't have a scale, how could you tell whether 4 apples are less than, greater than, or equal to 1 pound? Discuss it with your partner. Write or draw your answer.

(Answers may vary. One possible answer: Find something that weighs 1 pound, such as a 1-pound package of butter, and compare the weight of that object to the weight of the apples.)

27. TEMPERATURE

STANDARDS 2, 4, 10

Suppose you are standing outside looking at a Fahrenheit thermometer. The thermometer shows the temperature is 30°F. Does the air feel cold, cool, warm, or hot?

Draw a picture of the way you would dress to be outside in each of the following temperatures:
45° F   60° F
75° F   90° F

(Cold; check students' drawings. They should show clothing appropriate for cold weather [45°F], cool weather [60°F], warm weather [75°F], and hot weather [90°F].)

28. BELOW-ZERO TEMPERATURES

STANDARD 10

On a very cold winter morning, a Fahrenheit thermometer showed that the temperature was 6 degrees below zero. In the early afternoon the thermometer showed that the temperature was 25 degrees. How many degrees did the temperature rise? Draw a picture of a thermometer to help you find the answer.

(The temperature rose 31 degrees.)

Comparison Cards

1. _____

   IS AS TALL

   AS _____.

4. _____

   IS WIDER

   THAN _____.

2. _____

   IS SHORTER

   THAN _____.

5. _____

   IS THE SAME HEIGHT

   AS _____.

3. _____

   IS THE SAME LENGTH

   AS _____.

Measuring Squares

Figure 1

Figure 2

Number of Squares Used	Area	Perimeter

Measuring Objects

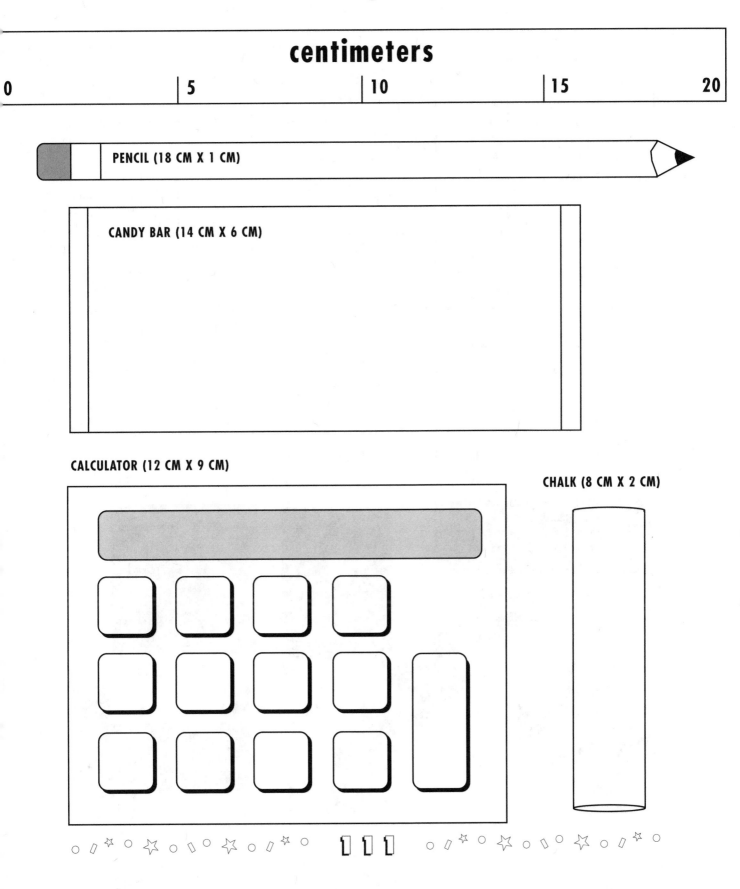

centimeters

| 0 | 5 | 10 | 15 | 20 |

PENCIL (18 CM X 1 CM)

CANDY BAR (14 CM X 6 CM)

CALCULATOR (12 CM X 9 CM)

CHALK (8 CM X 2 CM)

Area and Perimeter

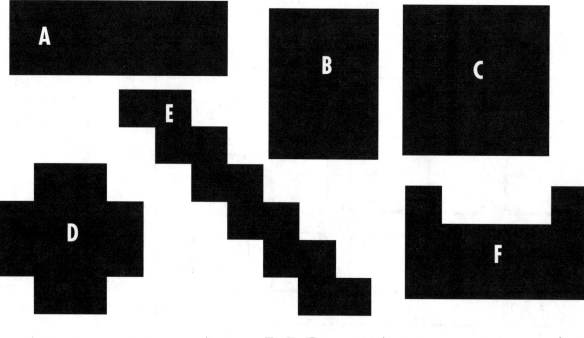

CHAPTER 11

Problem Solving

1. DESIGNING A 1-MINUTE WORKOUT

STANDARDS 1, 4, 5, 10

Sometimes we feel as though we've been sitting still too long, and we need to exercise our muscles. Work with a partner to create a 1-minute exercise workout. Make a plan to do at least 3 different exercises in that time. Estimate how many times you think each exercise can be done. Take turns timing and performing the exercise routine until you get the time down to 1 minute.

(Exercise routines will vary.)

2. SOLVING A NUMBER PUZZLE

STANDARDS 1, 6, 8

Complete the circle puzzle (page 119) following these directions. Write a number in each of the empty sections. The numbers must be placed so that each number is opposite a number which is double its value or half its value. The sum of all the numbers in the puzzle should be 36.

Compare your puzzle with your partner's. Make up a puzzle like this one.

Switch puzzles with your partner and solve.

3a. MAGIC SQUARE

STANDARDS 1, 8

In a magic square numbers are placed so that you get the same sum whether you add the numbers in a column, across a row, or diagonally from corner to corner. Complete the magic square, (page 119) so that there is a number from 1 to 9 in each box. Each number can be used only once.

6	1	8
7	5	3
2	9	4

3b. CREATING A MAGIC SQUARE

STANDARDS 1, 3, 8

Create your own magic square, writing the numbers from 1 to 9 in different boxes in the square. Remember, each number can be used only once. Explain how you decided where to place the numbers.

Write in 3 numbers from your magic square in their correct places in an empty magic square. Switch squares with your partner and solve.

(Magic squares will vary; methods students use to place numbers in the magic square will vary, but may include: guess and check; writing down all the combinations of 3 numbers less than 10 that have a sum of 15 and using that list to place the numbers in the square.)

4. FINDING ALL POSSIBLE COMBINATIONS

STANDARDS 1, 11, 13

Marcus, Alex, and Victor went on a picnic. They each brought some food. Altogether they had peanut butter sandwiches and cheese sandwiches, bananas and apples, bags of corn chips and bags of potato chips. Draw a picture to show the different lunches they could make if for each lunch they took 1 sandwich, 1 piece of fruit, and 1 bag of chips.

(Check students' drawings. They could make 2 x 2 x 2, or 8 different lunches.)

5. FINDING ALL POSSIBLE COMBINATIONS

STANDARDS 1, 11, 13

For this problem you need 5 different-colored slips of paper. Work with your partner to find how many ways you can arrange the slips of paper in 2 groups. A group can have 1 or more slips of paper in it. Draw pictures or make a table to record the different groups.

(There are 15 different ways to arrange the slips of paper into 2 groups—5 ways to have 1 slip of paper in one group and 4 slips in the other, and 10 ways to have 2 slips in 1 group and 3 slips in the other.)

6. LOGICAL THINKING

STANDARDS 1, 2, 3

What is wrong with this way of thinking?

If it snows, it's cold outside.
It isn't snowing.
Therefore, it isn't cold outside.

(Just because the statement "If it snows, it is cold outside" is true, does not mean its reverse—"If it isn't snowing, then it isn't cold"—is also true.)

7. LOGICAL THINKING

STANDARDS 1, 2

A boy and a girl are sitting next to each other. One of them has red hair and the other one has black hair. The one with black hair says, "I am a boy." The one with red hair says, "I am a girl." At least 1 of them is not telling the truth. Which one is the boy and which one is the girl? How do you know?

(The boy is the one with red hair, and the girl is the one with black hair. Possible answer: if 1 of them is not telling the truth, and says the opposite of what she or he means, then the other one must also not be telling the truth, since there is 1 boy and 1 girl.)

8. ODD AND EVEN NUMBERS

STANDARDS 6, 13

If the year you were born is an even-numbered year, and this year is an even-numbered year, will your age on your birthday this year be an odd or an even number?

If the year you were born is an odd-numbered year, and this year is an odd-number year, will your age on your birthday this year be an odd or an even number?

Will your age be an odd or even number if one of the years is an odd number, and one is an even number?

Write a rule you can use to tell for any year whether your age on your birthday that year will be an even or odd number.

(Even; even; odd. Possible rule: If birth year and calendar year are both odd or both even, the age will be an even number. If one of the years is odd and one even, the age will be an odd number.)

9. MEASURING PRECIPITATION

STANDARDS 1, 4, 8

Precipitation is the amount of water that falls on the earth. It takes about 10 inches of snow to equal the same amount of water as 1 inch of rain.

A C R O S S   T H E   C U R R I C U L U M

Logical Scenes (Language Arts)
Read the following problem about the cat, the mouse, and the cheese aloud and have children act out the solution.

A man had to take a cat, a mouse, and some cheese across a river in a boat. His boat was so small, though, he could only take 1 of them across at a time. He couldn't leave the cat alone with the mouse, or the mouse alone with the cheese. How could the man get all 3 across the river safely? How many trips across the river will it take?

(The man could take the mouse across, leave it on the opposite shore, then go back across and pick up the cheese. When he got the cheese across, he'd need to take the mouse back. Then he could pick up the cat and leave the mouse behind. Finally, he could go back across, pick up the mouse and bring it across again. It will take 7 trips across the river.)

If an area of land receives 30 inches of precipitation in a year, what are 5 different combinations of snow and rain it could have received?

(Answers will vary, but may include: 29 in. of rain, 10 in. of snow; 28 in. of rain, 20 in. of snow; 27 in. of rain, 30 in. of snow; 26 in. of rain, 40 in. of snow; 25 in. of rain, 50 in. of snow.)

10. CALCULATING TIME

STANDARDS 1, 3, 8, 10

At 1 water park, it takes 4 minutes to climb to the top of the water slide, and 1 minute to slide down it. Once they've landed in the pool below, people usually spend between 30 seconds and 2 minutes splashing around before getting out.

What is the greatest number of trips up and down the slide someone could make in 30 minutes? What other factors might you consider in calculating how many trips up and down the slide you could make in 30 minutes?

(Each trip up and down the slide can take from 5 minutes, 30 seconds to 7 minutes. The greatest number of trips you could make is 5—5 x 5 min, 30 seconds = 27 minutes; other factors to be considered may vary, but may include: whether or not you have to wait in line, whether you stop to talk or swim.)

11. FACT FAMILIES

STANDARDS 1, 7

Number fact families are made up of 2 or 3 numbers that together make at least 2 related number sentences. For example, 4, 25, and 100 are a fact family. The numbers can be used to make the following sentences: 25 x 4 = 100; 4 x 25 = 100; 100 ÷ 4 = 25; and 100 ÷ 25 = 4.

Choose 2 fact families and write the related sentences for each.

Write the numbers belonging to the 2 fact families in a mixed-up order. Switch papers with your partner. Separate the numbers into the 2 fact families and write their related sentences. Check each other's work.

(Fact families and related sentences will vary.)

12. ADDING FRACTIONS

STANDARDS 1, 10, 12

Look at the Letter Ruler (page 120). Each quarter of an inch is labeled with a letter of the alphabet. To find the value of a word, find where each letter of the word is located on the ruler and add the measures together. For example, the letter *I* is located at 2 1/4 inches; the letter *T* at 5 inches. So, the value of the word *it* equals 2 1/4 + 5, or 7 1/4 inches.

What is the value of your first name? Find a word that has a greater value than your first name. Find a word that has a lesser value than your first name. Write a number sentence for each.

(Number sentences and words will vary.)

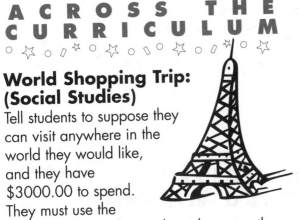

A C R O S S   T H E   C U R R I C U L U M

World Shopping Trip: (Social Studies)

Tell students to suppose they can visit anywhere in the world they would like, and they have $3000.00 to spend. They must use the money to buy a plane ticket, plus cover the cost of lodging and meals for a week. Students can research the cost of the trip and make up an expense log for it. In the log, students record how much their lodging costs each night, the price of the plane ticket, and the cost of each meal.

13. FINDING MEAN AND MODE

STANDARDS 1, 8, 11

Each student needs a penny. Follow the steps below to find the mode and mean for the number of years the students' pennies have been in circulation. Explain that you find the **mode** by identifying the value that occurs most often. Explain that you find an **arithmetic average,** or

mean, of a set of numbers by adding them and then dividing the sum by the number in the set. Both the mode and the mean are ways to describe an average value of a set of data.

a. Have each student find the number of years his or her penny has been in circulation by subtracting the year shown on the penny from the current year.

b. Make a graph of the results. Have students identify the number of years the greatest number of pennies have been in circulation. This is the **mode.**

c. Add the number of years of circulation together and divide by the total number of pennies. This is the **mean.**

Compare the mode and the mean.

(Mode and mean will vary with pennies used. The mean calculated may or may not have the same value as the mode; it also may or may not be a whole number.)

14. WRITING A PLAN FOR FINDING AN AVERAGE

STANDARDS 1, 2, 11

Write a plan for finding the average number of siblings of the students in your class.

(Plans should include a way to collect the data and discuss ways of finding either the arithmetic mean—adding the numbers of siblings and dividing by the number of students in the class, or the mode—identifying the number of siblings that is the same for the greatest number of students in the class.)

15. PROBABILITY

STANDARDS 1, 3, 11

Work with your partner to solve this problem. You may want to act out the solution.

It was dark in the morning when Jesse was getting dressed. He reached into his sock drawer, where he kept 10 pairs of white socks and 5 pairs of black socks. (Of course, they weren't together in pairs!) What is the fewest number of socks Jesse would need to pull out of his drawer before he could be positive he'd have two matching socks? Explain your answer.

(3 socks—the first sock he pulls out would be either white or black; the second sock might match the first sock, or it might not; the third sock will either match the first sock, the second sock, both socks, or neither sock, but in that case, the first 2 socks would have to match.)

16. PROBABILITY WITH NUMBER CARDS

STANDARDS 1, 3, 13

Magda and Bruce were playing with a set of cards numbered 1 to 24. "I'll bet I can pull a number greater than 20 out of this set of cards," said

Magda. "I have a better chance of pulling out an even number than you do of pulling out a number greater than 20," claimed Bruce. Was he right? Why or why not?

(Bruce was right. There are 4 cards greater than 20 in the deck of cards, so Magda has 4 chances out of 24 cards, or a 1:6 chance of pulling a number greater than 20. There are 12 cards with even numbers, so Bruce has 12 chances out of 24 cards to pull an even number from the deck, or a 1:2 chance.)

17. MAKING AND TESTING PREDICTIONS

STANDARDS 1, 11

Predict which vowel is used most often in our language. To check your prediction, count 100 words from 1 or more pages in a book. Work with your partner to make a tally of the number of times each vowel occurs in those 100 words. Which vowel occurs most often?

Repeat the activity for another set of 100 words. Does your answer change? How did your answer compare to your prediction?

(Predictions will vary; Results will vary, but most likely will show that the vowel e is used most often; comparisons will vary.)

NUMBER PUZZLES

**Circle
Puzzle**

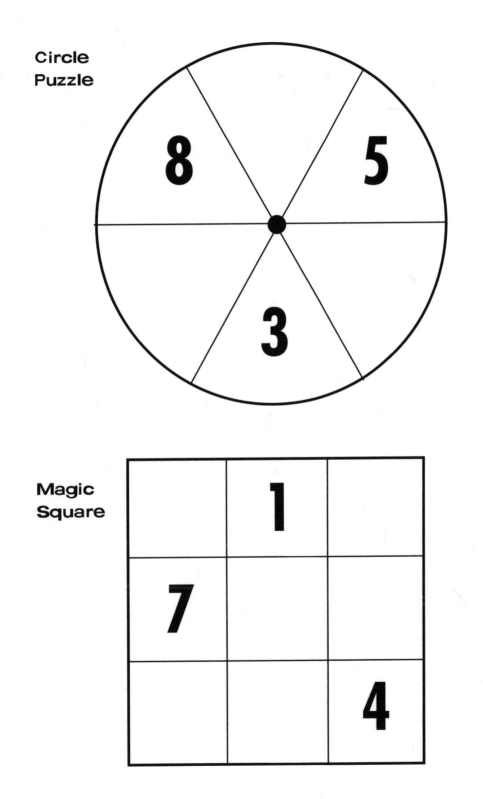

**Magic
Square**

Letter Ruler

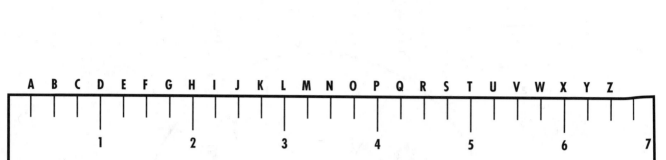